MW01115479

The Sacred Lotus and The Curi-ous Rabbit

Over 55 Buddhist Animal Wisdom Stories for Mindfulness, Positive Thoughts, Inner Peace and Happiness

By

Arya Kanan

Copyright © 2023 by Arya Kanan

All rights reserved. No part of this book may be reproduced or transmitted in any form or by any means, electronic or mechanical, including photocopying, recording, or by any information storage and retrieval system, without the written permission of the publisher or author, except in the case of brief quotations embodied in critical reviews and certain other noncommercial uses permitted by copyright law.

This book is published by BC Seminary Publishers.

Paperback Edition

First Edition: 2023

ISBN: 9789693292343

Contents

Forward

Welcome to a transformative journey that sets this collection apart from the multitude of other books. Prepare to delve into over fifty-five wisdom-laden narratives that transcend time, culture, and even your current understanding of life itself.

What sets this book apart? It's not merely a book; it's an intimate guide towards understanding the profound wisdom drawn from the ageless teachings of Buddha. But this isn't just about Buddha's wisdom. The stories span beyond the familiar narratives, bringing you unique lessons, like never seen before.

Unlike other books, these tales aren't confined to the realm of fiction or confined by the walls of academia. Instead, they present life's truths, cutting across the spectrum of human experience in the rawest form. Each story serves as a mirror, reflecting aspects of life that are often overlooked or forgotten in our busy lives.

The lessons encapsulated within these pages defy conventional teaching methods. They offer insights that you won't find in classrooms, teaching profound truths about joy, love, suffering, and the intricate tapestry of life.

This book promises more than just reading; it offers an experience. An experience of seeing the world through a prism of clarity, wisdom, and enlightenment. It invites you to witness the extraordinary nestled within the ordinary and challenges you to perceive life with renewed understanding.

In a world where books often replicate similar themes and teachings, this collection stands out, providing not just stories but life-altering experiences and wisdom. This is not just another book; it's a voyage of discovery, wisdom, and transformation. Are you ready to embark on this unique journey?

INTRODUCTION

Ladies and gentlemen, get ready for an adventure that started many, many years ago, back when I was just a student at a big school called University. I loved to paint and to learn about beautiful art from all over the world. That's when I discovered Buddhism, a way of life that is peaceful and teaches us to be aware of our thoughts and feelings. This journey led me to the Jataka tales, magical stories about the times the Buddha lived as different animals before he became a wise prince.

For years, these tales stayed tucked away in my mind, popping out when I least expected them. Just like a squirrel hides acorns for winter, these stories waited for the perfect time to reveal their wisdom. And one day, it struck me - why not bring these Buddhist animal stories to life through my art?

The journey wasn't easy - I took a big trip to India for three weeks in 2021 after the pandemic, hunting for more stories, creating sketches, and soaking in the incredible world around me. Like a treasure hunter, I discovered an old book with all 550 tales in a place where Buddha found enlightenment, which is like becoming a wisdom superhero!

Back home, I poured over the tales, selecting the best ones that would not only look cool as paintings, but also teach us valuable life lessons. It was tough, like choosing your favorite candy in a candy store. But finally, I picked 55 stories that felt just right.

Now, these tales might be ancient, but they've got a lot to say about life today. They talk about gratitude - being thankful for what we have. They highlight mindfulness - paying attention to the here and now. They preach self-love - understanding that we are all special in our own way. And above all, they teach us about happiness - finding joy in the simplest things.

So come along, let's dive into these tales, let's learn, laugh and discover together. They are going to change the way you think about life and help you appreciate the little things around you. Through the eyes of animals and the wisdom of the Buddha, we'll explore universal themes and timeless lessons. I hope you'll enjoy this journey as much as I enjoyed creating it for you! Get ready to be amazed, to feel grateful, mindful, and full of self-love and happiness. Let's turn the page, the adventure awaits!

The Lotus and the Serpent

In a forgotten corner of an ancient kingdom, nestled against the verdant backdrop of a dense forest, a placid pond took residence. The home of the deadliest serpent known in the land. Its scaled body shimmered ominously under the sun, and its piercing eyes sparked terror in every creature that crossed its path. Yet, this feared serpent was also the secret admirer of the lone lotus that resided on the surface of the pond.

The lotus, with its delicate petals unfolding in a resplendent display of purity, stood in stark contrast to the dread instilled by the serpent. One sunny day, the serpent slithered to the lotus, its curiosity piqued. It spoke in its sibilant voice, "Oh Lotus, why is it that despite sharing the same dwelling, you are revered while I am feared?"

The lotus, its pink petals glistening under the soft sunlight, responded serenely, "Dear Serpent, even though I am rooted in muddy waters, I strive to rise above it and bloom under the open sky. I absorb the sunlight and transform it into the beauty that you see. I radiate peace and symbolize purity amidst adversity. You, however, react to fear with fear, spreading your venom instead of tranquility."

This story illustrates the power of mindfulness, which is the ability to be fully present and engaged in our current situation without being overwhelmed. The lotus epitomizes mindfulness by remaining aware and unaffected by the murkiness below while focusing on blooming above the surface.

Like the lotus, we should aspire to maintain mindfulness in our own lives, acknowledging our present circumstances without letting them overshadow our potential for growth. We must recognize our environment, adapt, and persist, drawing on the energy around us to radiate peace and positivity.

Moreover, the story emphasizes gratitude, akin to the humble appreciation the lotus holds for the sunlight and the nourishment it derives from the water and soil. The lotus embraces its circumstances, thus transforming the seemingly unfavorable conditions into a source of life and beauty. In the same vein, we should show gratitude for the different elements of our lives, including the challenges, for they make our achievements even more worthwhile.

Finally, the tale resonates with the pursuit of happiness. The lotus finds joy in its tranquility and purity, symbolizing the importance of inner peace in the path to genuine happiness. Just as the lotus doesn't require validation from its surroundings, we must understand that true happiness springs from within us and is independent of external factors. It's about finding contentment in our own journey, appreciating our growth, and spreading the joy we harbor within us.

The Antelope Who Stood At Alert

Once upon a time, just outside the bustling city of Varanasi in India, a bright and lovely antelope made her home in a leafy forest, munching happily on the fruit that tumbled down from the trees, never bothering a single soul. However, the forest was also the hunting ground for a cunning hunter who made his living by hunting the creatures of the forest.

Now, this clever hunter had a nifty trick up his sleeve. He would build a hidden lookout in the treetops of fruit trees. When unsuspecting animals came to snack on the fallen fruits, BAM! They'd never know what hit them. They were used to scanning the forest floor for danger, not expecting threats from above.

One day, the hunter spotted a tree whose fruits were just ripening and dropping. Around the tree were the fresh tracks of an antelope and other signs of an animal's feast. So, the hunter decided to set up his treetop ambush there. He skillfully built a sturdy platform where he could stand, throw his spear with all his power, and still stay balanced. After erasing all traces of his activity, he left for the night.

Before the crack of dawn the next day, the hunter was already in his hideout, eyes keen and spear ready. As daylight filtered through the leaves, he spotted an antelope slowly approaching the tree. It was the same antelope who had been enjoying the tree's fruits for years. But as she neared the tree, she sniffed something odd in the air—a hint of human smell. She froze, trying to make sense of the scent.

The hunter noticed her hesitation and pondered his next move. To lure the antelope closer, he quietly tossed some ripe fruits toward her. But this only confirmed the antelope's suspicion. With her sharp eyes, she spotted the hunter concealed amongst the leaves. Deciding to tease him a little, she said, "Dear sepanni tree, something strange is happening today. Your fruit, which usually drop straight down, seem to be flying towards me. And instead of falling one by one, three have come at once without any wind. It seems you've forgotten how to be a tree, so I'll go find another one that hasn't!" With that, she began to move away.

This angered the hunter, and standing up in his hideout, he hurled his spear, which fell far short of the antelope. "Get out of here! You escaped today, but one day my spear will get you!" he shouted.

The antelope paused and gave the hunter some words to ponder, "Hunter, you might want to rethink your choices. Using tricks to harm the peaceful beings of the forest can only lead to harsh consequences in the end. Reflect on your actions today."

What to Learn From This Story

This story unfolds several important lessons that are quite relevant to our lives:

Firstly, the concept of intuition and awareness is highlighted through the antelope's
ability to sense danger and avoid the hunter's
trap. It reminds us of the importance of being
attentive and trusting our instincts in various
situations, as this heightened sense of awareness can protect us from potential harm.

The contrast between the hunter's cunning-
ness and the antelope's wisdom emphasizes
the value of wisdom over deceit and trickery.
The story encourages us to seek knowledge
and understanding rather than resorting to
dishonest tactics, as wisdom leads to better
outcomes and genuine connections with others.

Humor and wit are also showcased through
the antelope's clever retort to the hunter's attempt to deceive her. It demonstrates that
humor can be a powerful tool to disarm an
opponent or diffuse tense situations without
resorting to aggression.

The theme of Karma and consequences plays a significant role in the story. The antelope warns the hunter about the consequences of causing harm to others, emphasizing that our actions have repercussions. This encourages us to consider the impact of our behavior on others and strive for compassion and empathy in our interactions.

Lastly, compassion is exemplified through the antelope's final message to the hunter. Instead of retaliating with a threat, she offers advice out of concern for his well-being. This highlights the importance of treating others with compassion and understanding, even when faced with hostility or harm.

In conclusion, the story of the antelope and the hunter offers valuable insights into intuition, wisdom, humor, karma, and compassion. It encourages us to be mindful of our actions, seek understanding, and treat others with empathy and kindness.

The Parakeet That Under-stands Responsibilities

Once upon a time, nestled in the heartland of India, a vibrant flock of parakeets had their home in a cluster of kapok trees atop a hill. Their society was governed by a sagacious king and queen, who had birthed an extraordinarily stunning son whose beauty amplified with each passing season. As the royal couple grew older and frailer, unable to lead their community to lush feeding grounds, they passed this responsibility to their son. He accepted his new role with honor, promising to care for them just as they had nurtured him during his formative years.

Their habitat was surrounded by vast lands belonging to a prosperous landowner who had over a thousand acres sown with rice. Each fifty-acre plot was supervised by a separate caretaker. The lush rice fields at the base of the parakeet's hill were now ripe, attracting the young parakeet king who led his flock there for feasting. The assigned caretaker, unhappy about the birds eating the rice, tried to drive them away, but they would simply relocate within the field. Amid the flock, one parakeet caught his attention - the most magnificent bird that, after satiating its hunger, would gather a sizable amount of rice in its beak and fly away. Such behavior baffled the man, as he had never witnessed a parakeet collecting rice before.

As the parakeets continued to feed on the rice, the man grew anxious, fearing the landowner might blame him for the loss. He decided to inform his employer of the situation. The landowner, unperturbed by the birds feasting on his crop, was intrigued by the story of the rice-gathering parakeet. He instructed the man to catch this intriguing bird alive and bring it to him. Relieved that his employer was not bothered about the crop loss, the caretaker set a trap in the spot where the parakeet king usually fed.

The following day, the parakeet king unknowingly walked into the trap. His leg caught in the snare, he thought, "If I cry out now, the entire flock will scatter, missing their meal. I'll endure the pain until they've eaten, then raise the alarm." He did just that.

Once he was sure his flock had eaten their fill, he raised an alarm, causing the birds to fly away in fear, leaving him alone in the trap.

On hearing the commotion from his hut, the caretaker rushed to the snare, delighted to find the very bird he was tasked to capture. Tying the parakeet's legs together, he took the captured bird to the landowner, who carefully held the bird and asked, "Beautiful parakeet, why do you carry away beaks full of my rice? Do you own a farm or a granary? Or are you trying to retaliate against me?"

The parakeet replied with a tender voice, "Kind sir, I bear no grudge against you, nor do I own a granary or a farm. I am just fulfilling my duty. My parents, weak and old, depend on me for food. Out of my deep love for them, I bring back food, just as they did for me in my early days."

Touched by the parakeet's devotion and kindness towards his elderly parents, the landowner said, "Noble bird, your thoughts reflect love and respect." He untied the straps binding the bird's legs and applied soothing oils to the wounds caused by the trap. After feeding the parakeet some sweet corn and sugar water, he freed the bird, saying, "Return to your flock and your parents. You and your flock are free to feed from my fields anytime. You have taught me the true meaning of love and respect towards parents."

What to Learn From This Story

In the story of the parakeet king, several important themes and lessons are highlighted. One of the central themes is the idea of responsibility and duty. When the king's parents grow old and are unable to lead the flock, he steps up to take on the responsibility of leadership. This reflects the necessity of being responsible in every phase of life, whether it is in our family, community, or work.

Another significant lesson from the story is the importance of respect and care for the elderly. The parakeet king's devotion to his aging parents shows the value of treating the elderly with respect and providing them with the care and support they need. This echoes the universal principle of honoring those who have cared for us throughout our lives.

Patience and sacrifice are also emphasized in the story. The parakeet king endures the pain of the snare to allow his flock to eat their fill, illustrating the significance of being patient and making sacrifices for the well-being of others. This selflessness and concern for others' welfare are vital traits to cultivate in our own lives.

Kindness and empathy play a crucial role in the story as well. The landowner's response upon understanding the parakeet king's situation shows empathy and kindness. Instead of reacting harshly, he treats the parakeet with compassion and learns a valuable lesson from its actions. This highlights the importance of being kind and understanding towards all beings, even those different from us.

Lastly, the story underscores the idea that wisdom and learning can come from unexpected sources. The landowner learns a profound lesson about love and respect from the parakeet, demonstrating that we should always remain open to learning from all experiences and encounters. It reminds us that valuable insights can be gained from being receptive and open-minded.

In conclusion, the story of the parakeet king imparts important lessons about responsibility, respect for the elderly, patience, sacrifice, kindness, empathy, and the value of continuous learning and wisdom. These lessons serve as valuable guides for leading a compassionate and fulfilling life.

The Clever Rooster And The Cunning Falcon

In the historical Bamboo Grove near Rajgir in northeastern India, there once thrived a vibrant community of wild fowls. They enjoyed their tranquil lives, basking in the sun, foraging for meals amidst the meadows, and exploring the forest grounds. However, tranquility was disrupted by the arrival of a formidable falcon. His hunting prowess was unmatched, swooping down upon the wild fowl with lightning speed, snatching them with his mighty talons, and feasting upon them. The wild fowl's numbers dwindled rapidly, with nearly half their flock falling prey to the falcon.

A clever rooster, who served as the flock's leader, realized the need for a survival strategy. He began keeping the remnants of the flock within the confines of the dense bamboo grove. The bamboo's thick stalks and lush foliage created a protective barrier, prohibiting the swift falcon from snatching any more birds.

Despite his failed attempts, the falcon recognized the rooster's leadership and devised a scheme to lure the rooster into an open area. Once the rooster was out of the way, the falcon hoped to easily feast on the remaining birds.

The falcon perched on a nearby tree branch and addressed the rooster, "Noble fowl, I've been watching your dignified leadership and the significant influence you have on your flock. Fear me not, I only wish to befriend you. I'm aware of a place abundant with delicious seeds nearby. Join me and let's feast together as allies."

The rooster replied, "Magnificent hunter, it's impossible for a friendship to blossom between us. Depart from here, your companionship is unnecessary to me."

The falcon pleaded, "Honorable sir, I have transformed. I no longer prey on fowl; instead, I aspire to be their ally and guardian.

Grant me an opportunity to demonstrate my sincerity."

The rooster responded, "I've always believed in these principles—'Trust not those who spin tales, those guided by self-interest, or those that pretend excessive piety. Distrust those with fluctuating minds, as they are likely to waver once again. Do not trust the violent, as they may unleash their aggression upon you. Beware of false sweet words that lack sincerity, for they are meant to mislead.'

These principles guide me not to trust you, falcon. As long as you are in this vicinity, my flock and I will remain within this safe bamboo grove. Here, we have ample food and our lives are secure."

Recognizing the rooster's wisdom, the falcon realized he could not deceive him. With a disappointed heart, the falcon soared into the skies, seeking hunting grounds inhabited by less vigilant birds.

What to Learn From This Story

In this story, "The Wise Rooster and the Cunning Falcon," we are presented with a tale
that holds valuable lessons for us to ponder.
At its core, the story revolves around the
theme of wisdom and caution, as demonstrated by the rooster. This intelligent bird
teaches us that being vigilant and making
cautious decisions can shield individuals or
groups from potential threats and harm.

The rooster's character embodies the notion
of unchanging nature. It reminds us that the
inherent traits of individuals or things often
remain constant. In contrast, the falcon's nature as a predator does not change, and the
rooster is aware of this reality. This understanding leads the rooster to act prudently
and take necessary precautions when faced
with the falcon's persuasive claims of friendship.

The story also serves as a cautionary tale,
warning us about the dangers of false

pretenses. The falcon's sudden change of behavior and claims of reform should not be
trusted blindly. The rooster's distrust of the
falcon's intentions teaches us to be cautious
and discerning, especially when confronted
with individuals who seem to have transformed overnight.

Another crucial lesson from the story is the
importance of prudence over gullibility. It
urges us to engage in critical thinking and
question situations that appear too good to
be true. Instead of naively accepting things at
face value, we should carefully evaluate circumstances to make informed decisions.

Furthermore, the story sheds light on the
power of leadership. The rooster's role as a
leader plays a pivotal role in saving his flock
from the cunning falcon. It exemplifies how
good leaders prioritize the safety and well-
being of those they are responsible for.

In essence, "The Wise Rooster and the Cunning Falcon" serves as a reminder of the significance of wisdom, vigilance, discernment, and strong leadership in safeguarding ourselves and our communities from potential threats. By internalizing these valuable lessons, we can navigate life with greater prudence and protect ourselves from those who may wish us harm.

The Timid Elephant And Her Liberation From Fear

In a time long past, in a lush forest bordering an Indian kingdom just south of the majestic Himalayan range, there lived a splendid elephant. This creature was large and robust, young and full of life, with an unusually light skin tone that verged on white. Alongside her mother and the rest of the herd, she enjoyed the serenity of forest life, embodying a sweet yet shy demeanor.

However, the creature's alluring beauty and impressive size caught the eyes of the royal elephant trainers. They resolved to capture her for the king's amusement, and with the help of their own powerful elephants, they succeeded in their mission. The fair elephant was caught, a thick rope was looped around her neck, and she was hauled off to the king's training grounds. Enclosed in a log pen, she faced the harsh methods of the trainers, who sought to break her spirit and bend her to their will using whips and prods.

For many elephants, such methods were effective, but they instilled only terror in our delicate protagonist. Each trainer's visit incited panic within her, causing her to thrash against her pen. One day, in a state of fearful fury, she destroyed her enclosure and sprinted away.

Frantic and wild, the elephant fled to the valleys of the imposing Himalayas. She ran ceaselessly until she found herself deep within the mountains, beyond the reach of human civilization. Despite the search attempts of the king's men, the elusive elephant remained unfound and they eventually abandoned their quest. But even in the heart of the mountains, her fear remained, any sound — a gust of wind or the snapping of a twig — was enough to set her off, causing her to stampede through the valleys in terror.

Observing her plight was a wise old owl who resided in the same valleys. His heart filled with compassion for the terrified beast, the owl decided to confront her. Descending from his perch, he settled on a branch nearby, causing the elephant to pause in her panic. The owl gently reassured her, "Noble creature, fear me not. I am but a tiny bird, and I mean you no harm."

The owl's words gave the elephant pause, allowing him to continue: "You are safe here. The wind cannot harm you, and neither can anything else in this forest. You are its most formidable resident. There are no men here. The fear within you is your own creation, and it's this fear that is your only foe. However, you also possess the power to dispel it."

Touched by the owl's wisdom, the elephant responded gratefully, "Kind and sagacious owl, you have brought light to my fears. I thank you for your compassion." From then onwards, the elephant began to harness her fear. When an unfamiliar noise startled her, she paused, identified its source, and reminded herself not to be scared. Step by step, she began to reclaim control over her life from the clutches of fear.

What to Learn From This Story

This tale imparts several valuable lessons:

Power of Mind Over Fear: Fear, while natural, often comes from our mind and perception of the world rather than real, present danger. By acknowledging this, we can start to manage and even overcome our fears.

Wisdom and Perspective: The wise owl provides a different perspective, which the elephant didn't consider, illustrating how wisdom from others can help us see our problems in a new light and find solutions we may not have thought of.

Compassion and Understanding: The owl's empathy towards the elephant's plight demonstrates the power of compassion and understanding. It shows how extending kindness and wisdom can help others navigate their struggles.

Self-awareness and Change: The elephant's recognition of her problem and the decision to change her response to fear illustrates the importance of self-awareness and the willingness to change for personal growth and well-being.

In a broader sense, this story emphasizes the importance of emotional intelligence, empathy, and resilience, and shows that with patience and introspection, one can overcome internal struggles and fear.

The Benevolent Wood-pecker And The Ungrateful Lion

In the far reaches of a lush forest in North-western India, there existed a woodpecker known not only for its striking beauty but also for its peculiar eating habits. Unlike its kin who feasted on insects and worms, this woodpecker was a gentle soul who couldn't stand the thought of harming other beings, hence it survived on young plant shoots, flowers, and fruits. It was renowned in the forest for its amiable disposition and willing-ness to help fellow creatures.

One sunlit afternoon, the woodpecker was soaring high above the treetops when it dis-cerned a series of groans emanating from the earth. Curious, it swooped down to find the source: a lion, writhing in pain, lying list-lessly on the forest floor. Alighting on a nearby branch, the woodpecker inquired about the lion's plight. The lion confessed that a sharp bone was stuck in his throat, leading to immense discomfort and impend-ing death.

Without hesitation, the woodpecker sought a strong stick from the surrounding foliage. He persuaded the lion to open its jaws wide and lodged the stick between the formidable sets of teeth, keeping the lion's mouth agape. The courageous bird then flew into the lion's mouth, reaching the lodged bone. After much effort and delicate maneuvering, the bone dislodged. Triumphantly, the woodpecker carried the bone out with his beak, then removed the stick from the lion's mouth. The lion, relieved, thanked the woodpecker gruffly before retreating to recover, while the woodpecker, content at having helped, flew off to find its vegetarian delicacies.

Months later, a harsh drought hit the area, leaving the woodpecker deprived of food. Weakened by starvation, the bird spotted the lion he had saved earlier, feasting on a recently killed antelope. As the antelope was already dead, the woodpecker thought it permissible to consume a little of its flesh to survive. He cautiously approached the lion, hoping to be invited to partake in the meal. When no invitation came, the desperate bird finally asked for some meat.

To the woodpecker's surprise, the lion reacted harshly, warning him to keep away or be eaten himself. Feeling humiliated, the woodpecker sought solace on a tree branch overhead where an owl, having observed the entire incident, suggested revenge. However, the woodpecker, embodying kindness and wisdom, chose not to retaliate, insisting he hadn't helped the lion with the expectation of a return favor. His response moved the owl, who vowed to remember his lesson. Despite feeling hurt by the lion's ingratitude, the noble woodpecker, harboring no ill-will, flew away to search for sustenance elsewhere.

What to Learn From This Story

This story imparts several valuable lessons:

Compassion and Kindness: The wood-pecker displays kindness by helping the lion in distress, even though the lion is a much larger and potentially dangerous creature. This teaches the value of compassion towards all beings, regardless of their size, power, or status.

Selflessness: The woodpecker doesn't help the lion with any expectation of being rewarded in the future. This selfless act, done purely out of goodwill, shows the virtue of helping others without expecting something in return.

Wisdom and Forgiveness: When faced with the lion's ungratefulness, the wood-pecker doesn't seek revenge. Instead, he shows wisdom and forgiveness, teaching that harboring resentment or seeking retaliation doesn't lead to peace or satisfaction.

Courage: Despite being small and vulnerable, the woodpecker shows great bravery by entering the lion's mouth to remove the bone. This emphasizes that courage is not determined by size but by the willingness to face challenges and help others, even in potentially dangerous situations.

The Consequences of Ingratitude: The lion's ingratitude towards the woodpecker's help serves as a reminder of the importance of acknowledging and appreciating the kindness of others. Being ungrateful can lead to isolation and loss of potential allies.

The Hysterical Hare And The Wave Of Panic

Once Upon a Time, nestled in the lush out-skirts of Mumbai, India, lived a whimsical rabbit. He made a cozy burrow in the intertwining roots of a palm tree, surrounded by towering coconut trees. One tranquil day, while lounging beside his den and indulging in his daydreams, an absurd thought popped into his mind, "What would I do if the earth were to fall apart?"

No sooner had he pondered over this bizarre idea, a massive coconut plummeted from one of the lofty trees and landed with a resonating thud on a palm leaf right behind him. The ground quivered under the impact, and the unsuspecting rabbit, convinced his ridiculous imagination had become a reality, screamed, "The earth is collapsing!" Without a backward glance, he bolted, overcome by terror.

As the terrified rabbit dashed along the path, another curious rabbit hopped alongside, asking, "What's the matter? Is a jackal on your tail?" "Worse!" cried the panic-stricken rabbit, "The earth is disintegrating. Run for your life!" The two were soon joined by a multitude of rabbits, and the hysteria rapidly spread to the deer, boars, and buffalo. The rumbling crowd was further joined by an elephant and a rhinoceros. Thus, hundreds of animals, blindly gripped by fear, thundered across the plains towards the ocean.

High on a hill, a majestic lion, awakened by the cacophonous stampede, surveyed the pandemonium from his den. From his elevated perspective, he beheld an astounding spectacle: a diverse throng of terrified creatures charging towards the sea, without any visible cause. Sensing something amiss, he bravely positioned himself in the stampede's path, halting the frenzied crowd with three mighty roars.

Upon interrogating an exhausted elephant, the lion learned of the supposed 'end of the earth.' Tracing back the source of this wild rumor through buffalo, deer, and rabbits, he finally found the originator—the anxious rabbit who had mistaken a fallen coconut for a planetary disaster.

The lion, sensing the absurdity of the rabbit's tale, assured the anxious animals he would investigate the matter. Carrying the rabbit on his back, he retraced their steps to the origin of the scare. Finding a lone coconut amidst broken palm leaves, the lion quickly deduced the true nature of the 'end of the earth' sound.

Returning to the anxiously awaiting animals, the lion unveiled the truth—there was no threat to the earth. Relieved and somewhat embarrassed, the animals slowly made their way back home, the folly of their mass hysteria a reminder of the importance of not succumbing to panic without discerning the truth. The lion's bravery and wisdom had saved the day, teaching everyone a lesson about the dangers of blindly following the herd.

This story imparts several valuable lessons:

Avoid Hasty Conclusions: The rabbit's swift assumption that the earth was collapsing, based on a single event, led to a massive panic. This teaches us to avoid jumping to conclusions without adequate information or understanding.

Critical Thinking: It's crucial to analyze situations and use our reasoning skills before taking action. The animals' blind faith in the rabbit's claim almost led them into the sea, which could have ended tragically.

Don't Spread Unverified Information: The rabbit's fear quickly spread among other animals, leading to unnecessary panic. This highlights the importance of ensuring the information we pass on to others is accurate.

Leadership and Responsibility: The lion's role demonstrates good leadership. He managed to stop the panic, find out what was really happening, and relay that information back to the others. This is a crucial skill in crisis management.

Questioning the Herd Mentality: The story emphasizes the importance of independent thought. Just because "everyone" is doing something does not necessarily make it the right or best action.

Fear and Panic are Poor Advisors: Decisions made in a state of fear or panic are often irrational and can lead to unfavorable outcomes. It's important to remain calm and consider the situation carefully.

Wisdom In The Wild: Lessons From The Lion And The Rabbit

Many moons ago, in the verdant landscapes near Mumbai, resided a rabbit who was known for his daydreams. He lived under a palm tree, surrounded by towering coconut trees. One lazy afternoon, while lounging in the sun, the rabbit pondered, "What would happen if the earth were to shatter?"

As the thought crossed his mind, a coconut plummeted from a tree and crashed onto a palm leaf, creating a thunderous noise. Instantly, the rabbit concluded that the world was collapsing and he bolted away, consumed by fear. As he galloped, he encountered another rabbit to whom he shared his alarm. In no time, his fear had rippled through the animal kingdom, initiating a colossal stampede heading towards the sea.

Atop a hill, a lion heard the deafening sound of the stampede and was quick to notice the absence of any predator. The lion, recognizing that something was off, courageously positioned himself before the rushing horde and with three mighty roars, he halted the chaos.

Investigating the matter, the lion tracked the panic's origin to the rabbit. Listening to the rabbit's story, the lion was skeptical and decided to verify the claim himself. Returning to the site with the rabbit, he quickly discerned the truth behind the 'earth-shattering' noise — a fallen coconut.

Upon realizing the cause of the panic, the lion reassured the animals that the world was not ending and it was safe to return home. The majority of the animals felt sheepish for succumbing to herd mentality and not employing their common sense. The incident was a stark reminder that fear-induced decisions often lead to unfavorable outcomes and underscored the importance of critical thinking and leadership in crisis management.

Thus, the lion's sagacity and the rabbit's hasty assumption became a lesson for all animals: to think critically before acting, refrain from disseminating unverified information, and to remember that fear and panic are poor advisors. The tale served as a timeless reminder to question herd mentality and exhibit discerning judgment.

What to Learn From This Story

Gratitude: The story indirectly highlights the importance of gratitude by its absence. The animals later felt foolish for their hasty reactions, which could have led to disastrous results had it not been for the lion's intervention. This serves as a reminder to express gratitude to those who help us, like the lion who used his wisdom and courage to avert a catastrophe. Gratitude helps foster positive relationships and contributes to overall happiness.

Mindfulness: The rabbit's initial panic was the result of an absent-minded conclusion drawn from his imagination and an unconnected event - the falling of the coconut. This underscores the importance of mindfulness - being present in the moment and discerning the reality of a situation instead of letting our thoughts or fears distort our perception of events. Mindfulness can prevent needless anxiety and promote mental peace.

Happiness: Fear and panic spread quickly among the animals, causing them distress and almost leading them into disaster. The story thus illustrates how one's state of mind can heavily impact their happiness. By maintaining calmness, thinking critically, and not letting fear guide decisions, one can maintain a more positive outlook and achieve a greater sense of happiness. This tale emphasizes that happiness often comes from a state of peace and clarity, which can be cultivated through mindfulness and rational thinking.

The Unwise Adventure Of The Crows

In a time gone by, on the bustling coasts of the Arabian Sea near the grand city of Mumbai, there lived a pair of crows that scavenged along the coastal lands. They stumbled upon a makeshift altar one day, left behind from an offering ceremony to the sea gods, loaded with leftovers of milk, rice, meat, and potent liquor. Succumbing to their temptation, the crows heartily devoured it all, becoming inebriated from the strong liquor.

In their intoxicated state, they stumbled down to the water's edge, where they noticed seabirds frolicking in the waves. The male crow, in his drunken bravado, remarked to his mate, "Those sea birds strut about in the water as if they're superior. We can do just as well, don't you think?" To this, the female crow heartily agreed. In their drunken folly, they waded into the sea, trying to mimic the seabirds, laughing and splashing about. Suddenly, a shark broke the surface of the water, swiftly seizing the female crow in a single gulp.

Horrified, the male crow barely made it back to the shore. On the beach, he sat mourning, crying out loudly about the tragic loss of his wife to the unforgiving sea, conveniently leaving out their inebriated misadventure into the waters. A flock of crows gathered, drawn by his cries, to find out what had transpired.

Moved by his sorrow, one particularly naive crow proposed a seemingly heroic plan. He suggested they drain the sea by consuming its waters, to rescue their companion from her watery grave. The other crows, seeing some merit in this plan, began their futile endeavor, gulping down the salty seawater. However, they soon found their mouths parched, throats swelling, and jaws aching from the relentless drinking. As they collapsed, exhausted, on the sandy shores, one crow remarked, "It's impossible! Every gulp we take is replaced immediately. The sea is not going down at all."

They all agreed, abandoning their vain attempt at emptying the sea. Instead, they began to fondly remember the female crow, her captivating beauty, her radiant personality, her charming eyes. But before their elaborate tribute reached its peak, a looming storm cloud overhead unleashed a frightening flash of lightning and a thunderous roar, scattering the misguided crows in all directions.

What to Learn From This Story:

Drawing on the principles of Buddhism, we can glean several key lessons from this story:

Mindfulness: The crows, in their drunken state, lacked mindfulness, which is a fundamental principle of Buddhism. Their thoughtless decision to enter the sea led to the tragic loss of life. This emphasizes the importance of being present and mindful in our decisions and actions.

Craving and Attachment: The crows' craving for the offerings and subsequent attachment to the idea of emptying the sea led to suffering. This relates to the Buddhist principle that desire and attachment can lead to suffering (Dukkha) and the cause of suffering (Samudaya).

Non-Harming (Ahimsa): The crows' act of consuming liquor and their foolhardy attempt to enter the sea resulted in harm to themselves and others, which violates the Buddhist principle of non-harming.

Wisdom and Discernment (Prajna): The crows lacked the wisdom to understand the consequences of their actions and the discernment to tell right from wrong. They didn't have the wisdom to realize the futility of their attempt to empty the sea.

Impermanence (Anicca): The crows' experience serves as a stark reminder of the Buddhist principle of impermanence, which asserts that all conditioned existence, without exception, is transient, or in a constant state of flux. The death of the female crow is a stark example of this.

Compassion (Karuna): Even though their methods were misguided, the crows did display a sense of compassion for their lost companion by attempting to empty the sea and later praising her. This highlights the importance of compassion in Buddhism.

The Middle Way: The crows indulged excessively in the offerings, particularly the liquor. This extreme behavior led to poor judgment and tragic consequences. Buddhism espouses the Middle Way, a path of moderation away from the extremes of self-indulgence and self-mortification.

Through these principles, the story teaches us to practice mindfulness, understand the nature of our desires and their potential to cause suffering, exercise wisdom in our decisions, respect the impermanence of life, and cultivate compassion while avoiding extremes in our behaviors.

The Beetle And The Elephant

Once upon a time, there was a rest stop smack dab in the middle of two towns in India. Travelers would hang out there, have dinner, and sometimes, sip on their sodas a bit too much. One day, a tipsy traveler spilled his root beer, and it pooled in a crevice on a rock.

Along came a dung beetle, drawn to the rest stop by the smell of horse poop from the traveler's horses. He found the root beer spill, gave it a taste, and boy, did he love it! He drank till his belly was full, and then...he was not feeling quite himself.

He was walking weird, stumbling around in horse poop and mud. He even fell into the mud! But instead of feeling silly, he said, "Wow, I'm so strong, the whole world can't even handle how heavy I am!"

Just then, a big ol' elephant was walking to the river for a sip of water. The elephant saw the wobbly beetle rolling around in horse poop and thought, "Maybe I should take a detour." As the elephant turned around, the beetle saw him and shouted, "Hey, Mr. Elephant! Are you scared of me? Come back and let's see who's stronger!"

The elephant, realizing the beetle was all silly from too much root beer, decided to teach him a lesson. "Alright, Mr. Beetle," he said, "I accept your challenge, and I get to choose what we'll use to fight."

And with that, the elephant turned around, lifted his tail, and dropped a massive pile of elephant poop right on the beetle. "Looks like you're in your favorite place now, Mr. Beetle. I think I won." The elephant then walked to the river, quenched his thirst, and strolled back to the forest, leaving the silly beetle squirming under a mountain of poop.

What to Learn From This Story:

Firstly, let's address gratitude. The beetle in the story was so caught up in the root beer that he failed to appreciate his surroundings and the simple pleasures of his existence. If he had paused to be thankful for the peaceful life he was leading, he might have avoided the whole messy situation with the elephant. This story encourages us to appreciate the good in our lives before seeking out unnecessary complications.

Next, there's mindfulness. This quality is all about being fully engaged with the present moment. The beetle certainly wasn't being mindful when he consumed so much root beer and then foolishly challenged an elephant. If we practice mindfulness in our daily lives, staying aware of our actions and their potential consequences, we can make better decisions and avoid unnecessary difficulties.

The third theme is self-love. This story clearly shows that the beetle didn't demonstrate self-love. By overindulging and neglecting his own well-being, he ended up in a situation that was both embarrassing and dangerous. Self-love means respecting ourselves enough to make healthy choices and to stay safe. It reminds us that we are worthy of care and consideration, just as much as anyone else.

Finally, the story brings us to happiness. The beetle mistakenly thought that drinking root beer and showing off would bring him joy. Instead, he wound up covered in elephant dung. True happiness isn't about boasting or proving ourselves to others. Rather, it comes from within, from appreciating the simple moments, practicing mindfulness, and demonstrating love for ourselves.

In conclusion, this engaging story serves as a reminder that life is best enjoyed when we express gratitude, stay mindful of our actions, show love to ourselves, and seek out authentic happiness. The unfortunate beetle learned these lessons the hard way, but we can take them to heart and apply them to our lives without having to find ourselves in a similar predicament.

The Bufalo And The Monkey

Once upon a time, right on the edge of a big city called Gaya in India, a super strong buffalo lived in a lush green forest. This buffalo was seriously impressive, like a living, breathing tank with sharp horns, muscles upon muscles, and a shiny dark blue coat. He was so strong that even the lions and tigers gave him space!

But even though he looked tough on the outside, he was actually super nice on the inside. He was a gentle giant and a pretty wise one at that. A little monkey living in the forest found out about the buffalo's sweet nature and thought it'd be fun to play tricks on him.

This monkey was a total goofball. He'd climb onto the buffalo's back and pretend he was in a rodeo, he'd do crazy acrobatics swinging from the buffalo's horns, and sometimes he'd cover the buffalo's eyes just for kicks. He'd even jump on the buffalo's head while he was sleeping just to wake him up, or poke his ears with a stick. No matter what the monkey did, the buffalo just shrugged it off, never seeming to get bothered by it. The monkey was having a blast, always thinking up new ways to get on the buffalo's nerves.

An owl who lived in the same forest watched all this go down, and she was pretty confused. One day, she just had to ask the buffalo, "Hey there, Mr. Buffalo, you're the big guy around here. Even the tigers and lions are scared of you. So why do you let this silly monkey mess with you like that? You could put a stop to his tricks in a heartbeat. Why don't you?"

The buffalo looked at her, blinked slowly, and then said, "You know, I'm well aware of how strong I am. But, why should I use my strength against that little monkey? It's easy-peasy to be nice and patient with those who are good to you. The real test is being patient and kind to those who are not so nice. This monkey, with all his tricks, is actually doing me a favor. He's helping me practice patience and kindness. Whether he learns from me or not, that's up to him. It's not my job to discipline him. We all need challenges to grow better. This monkey is my challenge, my chance to become even more patient and kind."

The owl was awestruck. She nodded and said, "Your greatness, Mr. Buffalo, is not just about your size, but your incredible wisdom too. Thanks for teaching me such a cool lesson." And off she went back to her treetop, deep in thought over the buffalo's wise words.

What to Learn From This Story:

First let's talk about compassion; The buffalo displays immense compassion for the monkey, despite the monkey's mischievous actions. Even when the monkey is being annoying, the buffalo chooses understanding and patience. Just like the buffalo, we can try to empathize with people around us, even if they are making our life a bit difficult. Compassion makes us kinder and more understanding.

Secondly non-violence; the buffalo knew about his own strength but he didn't use it to harm the monkey. This is a classic example of the Buddhist principle of non-violence or 'Ahimsa'. We should always try to avoid causing harm to others, either through our words or actions.

Another is patience. One of the most important qualities the buffalo showed was patience. Even though the monkey kept bothering him, the buffalo remained calm and patient. Patience helps us to deal with the ups and downs of life without losing our cool.

Lastly, wisdom; the buffalo knew that the monkey was providing him an opportunity to grow his virtues, to become more patient, compassionate, and understanding. Recognizing this is a sign of wisdom. In life, we often face situations that test us, but if we look at them as opportunities to grow, just like the buffalo, we can gain wisdom.

So this story is all about learning compassion, practicing non-violence, having patience, and gaining wisdom. We can apply these teachings in our everyday life to make it more peaceful and fulfilling. It's just like the buffalo said, we all need challenges to develop our virtues!

The Elephant And The Dog

A while back in the bustling city of Varanasi, the king had a big herd of elephants. His most cherished one had an unusual buddy — a little dog. The dog first showed up at the elephant's stable to munch on the rice that slipped from the elephant's mouth during meal times. As days rolled into weeks, the elephant and the dog became inseparable pals. The elephant wouldn't touch her food unless her little friend was there to share it with her. They did everything together - sleeping, bathing, and even playing, with the elephant gently tossing the dog around with her trunk.

But then, one day, a mean stable worker sold the dog to a random traveler for a few coins. After her friend was gone, the elephant was super sad. She stopped eating, drinking, and bathing. She just stood in her corner, swaying back and forth with sorrow. When the king found out about his favorite elephant's worsening condition, he was really worried. He summoned his smartest advisor and said, "Check on my dear elephant and figure out what's wrong with her."

The advisor did a thorough check-up and found nothing physically wrong with the elephant. So, he figured that it must be something emotional. He asked the elephant's main caregiver, "Did anything change in the stable recently?"

The caregiver replied, "Indeed, the elephant had a close friend in a dog, but the dog disappeared some time ago."

Hearing this, the advisor hurried back to the king and reported, "Your elephant is very upset because her dog friend is gone."

"Well," said the king, "how in the world am I going to find a lost dog in this gigantic city?"

"I suggest making a public announcement that anyone found keeping a dog from the king's elephant stable will have to pay a hefty fine," advised the advisor.

The king did exactly that. The traveler who bought the dog heard about the king's announcement and instantly let the dog go. The dog, quick as a flash, darted back to the elephant's stable.

As soon as the dog returned, the elephant was so happy that she shed tears of joy. She gently picked up the dog with her trunk and cuddled it. She waited until her little friend had been fed; then, she too gobbled up her food. In no time, she was back to her usual cheerful self, with her loyal doggie friend always by her side.

What to Learn From This Story:

This delightful tale shares several important lessons for both children and adults, teachings often aligned with Buddha's philosophy of kindness, empathy, and the power of friendships.

Firstly, it tells us about the importance of companionship and love. Regardless of their size or species, the elephant and the dog developed a profound bond, reminding us that friendship knows no boundaries. This resonates with Buddha's teachings on "Metta" or universal love, highlighting the need to extend kindness and friendship to all beings.

Secondly, the story demonstrates the strength of emotional connections and how they can deeply affect us, animals or humans. When the dog was sold, the elephant experienced what can be understood as depression, illustrating the profound impact our relationships have on our emotional wellbeing.

Lastly, it serves as a reminder about empathy and compassion. The king's advisor, instead of dismissing the elephant's sorrow, took time to understand her emotional distress, and the king acted upon it, reflecting the Buddha's teachings on Karuna (compassion) and the importance of understanding and addressing others' suffering.

These lessons can be a guide for children and adults alike, reminding us of the deep bonds of friendship, the importance of emotional well-being, and the practice of compassion in our everyday lives.

The Glittering Duck

A long time ago, tucked away in a forest in India, there lived a pretty spectacular duck. But he wasn't just any duck – he was golden! Not just gold-like, but made of real gold. He shone like a tiny sun, lighting up everything around him. Being super smart, he knew humans could get a little too excited about gold, so he made sure to stay out of their sight.

Near his favorite chill spot in the forest, there was this small hut. Inside lived a mom and her two daughters. They didn't have much, but they were full of kindness, and the duck found himself really liking them.

One day, when the girls were outside playing, the duck flew over and landed right on their roof. The girls were thrilled, "Mom, come see this awesome duck on our roof!" Mom came out and couldn't believe her eyes.

The duck, feeling chatty, said, "I see you're having a tough time. How about I help you out? Every now and then, I'll give you one of my golden feathers. You can sell it to buy food and clothes." And with that, he gave them a shiny feather. They were over the moon, and over the next few months, the duck kept his promise. The family's life changed drastically – they never went hungry, and they all got to wear new clothes.

But one day, mom got a little greedy. She told her girls, "What if our duck friend decides to bail one day? We should grab him the next time he visits, pluck out all his feathers, and be the richest family around!"

The girls were horrified at the thought of hurting their kind friend, but when the golden duck came by next, mom caught him. She plucked out all his golden feathers and shoved him in a barrel. Then something crazy happened – the plucked feathers turned into regular gray and brown duck feathers. By trying to steal all at once, mom had ruined the magic.

Mom was disappointed, thinking of the fortune she'd lost, but the girls cried for their friend. Though he couldn't fly, he was still alive. They took care of him, shared their food, and helped him get better. Over time, he grew new feathers – not gold, just ordinary duck feathers.

What to Learn From This Story:

Once he was back on his feet, he decided to join a flock deep in the forest. He felt bad about leaving the girls but didn't want to be around humans anymore, having seen what greed can do. But he promised to drop by and visit every now and then.

From "The Glittering Duck", we can learn some valuable lessons:

Kindness Goes a Long Way: The golden duck showed kindness to the family out of the goodness of his heart, demonstrating that being kind can make a big difference in people's lives.

Greed Can Be Destructive: The mother's greed led to the loss of the golden feathers and caused harm to the duck. This illustrates the damage that greed can cause.

Respecting Boundaries is Important: The golden duck gave his feathers willingly and on his terms. When the mother forcefully took all the feathers, she crossed a line, leading to negative consequences.

Caring for Others is Rewarding: The girls showed empathy towards the duck, taking care of him and nursing him back to health. This portrays the importance and rewards of caring for others, even when they can't give you anything in return.

Material Wealth Isn't Everything: In the end, the golden duck chose to live away from human society, hinting at the idea that material wealth isn't as important as peace and kindness.

Greed Leads to Loss: The family had a good thing going with the golden duck giving them feathers. But the mother's impatience and greed led to their loss. Sometimes, it's best to appreciate and be grateful for what we have.

The Eagle And The Quail

Once upon a time, there was a young quail dwelling in the farmland outskirts of the magnificent city of Varanasi. This quail spent his days hopping on the fresh furrows made by the farmer's tillage, relishing the delicious morsels turned up by the toiling farmer. The furrows were soft when freshly tilled, but the intense Indian sun soon hardened them like stones.

The quail's kin had always scavenged these fields for sustenance, and his father had imparted to him the skills necessary to locate the choicest seeds and how to forage cautiously. One sweltering day, the young quail grew weary of his habitual hopping in the intense sunlight. He recalled stories of the forest's edge, where the sun's heat was lessened by the cooling shade and where plentiful seeds were available. Intrigued, he took flight towards the forest. True to the tales, he discovered a profusion of seeds and was sheltered from the sun by the high trees. He dined so eagerly that he failed to observe a sharp-eyed eagle perched on a barren branch on the forest's edge, keeping a close watch on everything below. However, the eagle had taken note of him, launched himself into the sky, gained altitude, and silently descended, seizing the unsuspecting quail with his razor-sharp talons. The eagle planned to enjoy his new catch as a delightful supper on his favorite roost.

To ensure the eagle could hear, the quail exclaimed, "How foolish I have been! I should never have ventured here to dine. This was a reckless error. Had I remained in my customary area, this eagle wouldn't have had a chance to ensnare me."

Hearing the chuckle from the smug eagle, he added, "Indeed, if I had been in my territory, I would have stood my ground against this formidable bird."

Laughing uncontrollably, the eagle questioned the quail, "Pray tell, where would a quail be a match for an eagle?"

"In the exposed tilled field where my father educated me to forage, Noble Eagle," the quail replied.

Laughing uproariously, the eagle said, "You, a contender for me in an open field! I must witness this for myself. I shall set you free, and we will have our contest in the field."

With that, the eagle released the quail, who quickly flew back to the tilled field that was his familiar feeding ground. He found a massive, rock-hard dirt clump that provided good cover at its rear.

The eagle circled above while the quail shouted, "I am ready for you, Mr. Eagle." The eagle dived with all his might at the courageous little quail who stood tall and proud on the large, hard dirt clump. The quail held his ground until the last second before the eagle made contact, then he swiftly retreated beneath the clump. The powerful eagle collided with the hard clump with such force that it knocked him unconscious.

The quail hopped back onto the clump and reflected, "Indeed, what my father always taught me holds true: we are always safest on familiar ground."

What to Learn From This Story:

This story provides several valuable life lessons:

Familiarity Provides Advantage: We are often at our strongest and most capable when in familiar surroundings or situations. This is because we understand the nuances and characteristics that can be turned to our advantage. The quail knew how to utilize the hardness of the furrow clods for his own protection against the hawk.

Respect Boundaries: There are often good reasons for boundaries in the natural world and in human society. Straying too far from what we know and where we belong can expose us to dangers we are not prepared to handle, just as the quail found when he ventured into the forest.

Beware of Overconfidence: The story warns against underestimating others and overestimating one's own abilities. The hawk's arrogance and dismissal of the quail's abilities led to his downfall.

Use Your Unique Skills: Each creature or individual has unique skills and knowledge that can help them survive and thrive. The quail's intimate knowledge of its habitat and its ability to react quickly helped it survive the attack.

Importance of Listening to Elders/Wise Counsel: The wisdom of the quail's father helped him survive a dangerous situation. This teaches us the importance of listening to and learning from those with more experience.

The Ignorant Monkeys

In the lush recreational gardens of Varanasi's monarch, there resided a merry band of monkeys. They led an untroubled existence, blessed with plentiful sustenance and devoid of peril. However, one day, the park's caretaker, intending to partake in a week-long citywide festival, was worried about the recently sowed saplings that required watering in four days. The gardener surmised that even the monkeys could handle a task as straightforward as watering the trees, so he enlisted their aid during his absence.

Approaching the alpha monkey, the gardener noted the monkeys' fortunate circumstances of living in the park and requested their assistance with the watering. The monkey leader, more than happy to help, agreed. Feeling assured, the gardener provided them with watering pots and set off for the festival.

The monkey chief was diligent in keeping time, and on the fourth day, he assembled his troops, distributed the watering pots, and directed them to water the saplings. The monkeys, filled with excitement, ran amok, splashing water over the trees' foliage, resulting in hardly any water seeping into the soil. The leader understood the roots were the focus, but he was unsure about the appropriate quantity of water. Consequently, he regrouped the monkeys and proposed, "To determine the accurate amount of water for the saplings, we should unearth each tree to assess the length of its roots. We'll allocate more water to those with elongated roots and lesser to those with shorter roots."

"An ingenious concept," responded the other monkeys, and off they dashed, yanking out each sapling that the gardener had painstakingly planted.

Naturally, the amount of water given to the roots was inconsequential. The young saplings, traumatised by the abrupt uprooting, started to wither and die instantly.

Meanwhile, two of the king's counsellors, while wandering through the park, witnessed the bizarre antics of the monkeys. One of them confronted a monkey in the act of up-rooting a tree and inquired about his actions.

The monkey, eager to explain, said, "In the gardener's absence, he asked us to help with the watering, and we're simply executing our wise leader's orders to water the trees based on their root lengths."

One counsellor commented to his associate, "This serves as a perfect illustration of how well-meant intentions can have calamitous outcomes when executed by those lacking adequate knowledge or wisdom."

The other advisor concurred, "Indeed, it also makes one question the wisdom of the gar-dener who would entrust such an important task to monkeys in the first place."

What to Learn From This Story:

There are a few key lessons to learn from this story:

Good Intentions are Not Enough: The monkeys had good intentions when they decided to help the gardener, but because they didn't have the right knowledge or understanding of how to properly water the trees, their actions led to negative consequences. This shows that good intentions need to be paired with correct knowledge and wisdom for effective action.

Task Suitability: Assigning tasks should take into account the abilities and understanding of those who are assigned. The gardener misjudged the capabilities of the monkeys, leading to the destruction of his saplings. It's a reminder that responsibilities should align with the skills and knowledge of the individual or team involved.

Importance of Communication and Understanding: The gardener failed to clearly communicate to the monkeys how to water the trees. The monkeys, in turn, didn't fully understand the task. This resulted in a misunderstanding and a failed task. Clear communication and comprehension are vital in any task's success.

Consequences of Ignorance: The monkeys' ignorance about the proper care of saplings led to the saplings' death. This underscores the potential harm that can come from a lack of knowledge or understanding. It stresses the importance of education and learning in any undertaking.

The Cunning Fox And The Vanity-Driven Raven

Once upon a time, on the periphery of the majestic city of Varanasi, a splendid grove filled with rose-apple trees existed. A crow was perched on a lower branch of one such tree, basking in the sun while delighting in the succulent apples.

A jackal, in search of a meal, happened upon the grove. He noticed the crow perchedo high above, relishing the fruit that was tantalizingly beyond his grasp. An idea sparked in the jackal's mind, "Crows are often susceptible to flattery. If I indulge this bird's vanity, it may toss some of those delectable apples down to me."

He began his flattery loud enough for the crow to hear, "Oh, what melodious sounds are these that reach my ears? Could it be the serenade of the sweetest songbird? The tender lullaby that caresses my soul is nothing short of magical. As I lift my eyes to its source, I am astounded by your magnificent beauty, superior to even the peacock's grandeur. Your vibrant feathers, noble stature, and illustrious lineage make you the most splendid bird I have ever had the privilege of beholding!"

Blinded by the jackal's untruths, the crow puffed his chest in pride. He responded, "Only one with a noble lineage can recognize the nobility in another. I see in you the elegance and majesty of a young tiger. Allow me to share some of this exquisite fruit with you." The crow then rustled the branches causing a cascade of ripe apples to rain down on the cunning jackal, who savored the rewards of his clever ruse.

What to Learn From This Story:

A wise owl, perched in an adjacent tree, had watched the entire exchange. She shook her head disapprovingly and remarked, "A pair of scavengers, feeders on refuse and carrion, yet they flatter each other as if they are royalty. Despite the sweetness of the fruit around me, this spectacle leaves a bitter taste." Disgusted, she took wing to seek peace in a different part of the forest.

1. **Beware of Flattery**: The crow was deceived by the jackal's flattery, demonstrating that we must be careful not to let flattery cloud our

judgement or distract us from a person's true intentions. Flattery is often used by people to manipulate others for their own benefit.

2. **Understand Your Worth**: The crow let the jackal's flattering words inflate his ego. It's crucial to have a realistic understanding of our worth and not let others' compliments or criticisms alter our self-perception.

3. **Wisdom over Folly**: The owl represents wisdom in this story, not falling for the superficial and shallow interaction between the crow and the jackal. This suggests that wisdom and discernment are valuable traits that can help us see beyond surface-level interactions.

4. **Honesty is the Best Policy**: The jackal used dishonesty to achieve his goal, which might work in the short term but will likely lead to mistrust and conflict in the long term. Being truthful and honest is usually a better approach.

5. **Reflect on the Quality of Interactions**: The owl was disgusted by the interaction between the jackal and the crow. This serves as a reminder to reflect on the quality of our relationships and interactions - are they based on genuine respect and understanding or manipulation and deception?

Granny's Faithful Companion

Once upon a time, in a modest hamlet located in the outskirts of the majestic city of Varanasi, an impoverished elderly widow resided. Her brother had once offered assistance to a man of affluence in the city. As a token of gratitude, he bequeathed an array of rare presents to the brother's family. To the elderly woman, he gifted a baby elephant. Her heart swelled with joy as she took the elephant under her wing, raising it as her own. She tirelessly fed it rice and porridge, working strenuously to fulfill the burgeoning appetite of the growing beast.

The elephant, affectionately named Blackie by the village children due to its unusually dark color, seamlessly integrated into the village community. Blackie quickly became a beloved playmate for the children, offering rides on his back, swinging them playfully with his trunk, and splashing them with water at the riverbank.

One beautiful day, Blackie beckoned Granny to accompany him to the river. To this, Granny replied, "Oh, Blackie, I'd love to join you, but my chores beckon me." For the first time, Blackie noticed the toilsome life Granny led to support them both while he spent his days frolicking with the children. He pondered over this realization and resolved to find some work to alleviate Granny's burden.

While at the river the following day with his youthful companions, a caravan owner arrived at the riverbank. His oxen struggled to haul his five hundred heavily laden carts across the rough riverbed towards Varanasi. The urgency to deliver the goods to the city was high, for delay meant substantial financial loss. Spotting the robust elephant by the river, he inquired about its ownership. The children promptly replied, "He's Granny's companion, and we call him Blackie."

Intrigued, the man proposed, "I offer two coins for every cart Blackie hauls across the river." Overjoyed at this prospect, Blackie accepted the task. One by one, he tugged the carts across the challenging river terrain. It was laborious but Blackie's strength prevailed, successfully transporting all five hundred carts across the river.

With the task completed, the caravan owner presented a bag containing five hundred coins and fastened it around Blackie's neck. Sensing the discrepancy, Blackie knew the bag did not contain the promised one thousand coins. In silent protest, Blackie reclined at the head of the caravan, refusing to budge until he was justly compensated. Recognizing Blackie's awareness, the owner rectified his mistake by adding the remaining five hundred coins.

Exhausted but triumphant, Blackie, with the children trotting alongside, returned home. Covered in dust and mud, his bloodshot eyes a testament to his strenuous exertion, he was greeted by a worried Granny. Observing Blackie's state and the heavy bag around his neck, Granny exclaimed, "Oh, Blackie, what ordeal have you endured? And what's that around your neck?"

Upon hearing the tale of Blackie's labor and his insistence on being fairly compensated, Granny swelled with pride. Together with the children, she led Blackie to the river for a well-deserved bath. That evening, she prepared an extra helping of Blackie's favored dish. From that day forward, Blackie continued to find occasional work, providing a comfortable life for himself and Granny. Her remaining years were thus spent in peace and comfort, thanks to her loyal companion, Blackie.

What to Learn From This Story:

1. **Empathy and Responsibility**: Blackie, the elephant, recognized the efforts Granny was putting into taking care of him. This led him to find ways to ease her burden. The story emphasizes the importance of being empathetic towards those around us and taking responsibility to help when we can.

2. **Honesty and Integrity**: When Blackie was underpaid, he refused to move until he received the correct amount. This shows the significance of standing up for what is right, demonstrating integrity even when others might be dishonest.

3. **The Value of Hard Work**: Blackie undertook a difficult task to help Granny, illustrating that hard work is often necessary to achieve our goals or to help those we care about.

4. **Appreciation and Care**: Granny showed her appreciation for Blackie's efforts by taking care of him after his hard work. It's important to express our gratitude and reciprocate when others do good things for us.

5. **Fairness and Justice**: The story also highlights the importance of fairness and justice. Blackie made sure that he was compensated fairly for his work, demonstrating that everyone should be given their due respect and reward.

6. **Mutual Support**: The story emphasizes the value of mutual support and co-dependence in relationships, as seen in the relationship between Granny and Blackie. They both looked after each other's needs, demonstrating a strong bond and mutual respect.

The Benevolent Mouse

Once upon a time, not far from the city of Varanasi in Northwest India, there was a deserted village where a kind-hearted mouse lived in a long-forgotten mansion. The mansion was once owned by a prosperous merchant who had stashed an immense treasure of gold coins underneath the floorboards and passed away without revealing this secret to anyone. The mouse, who had discovered the treasure, had no use for gold and continued her usual routine of scavenging for food.

Not far from the village, an old stone quarry was still being worked by a solitary stonecutter. The mouse would often observe the young man from afar, admiring his humble nature and hard work. Remembering the hidden fortune beneath her dwelling, she decided that the kind-hearted stonecutter was deserving of the wealth. Thus, she took a gold coin and presented it to him.

The stonecutter, surprised at the sight of a mouse carrying a gold coin, exclaimed, "Mother Mouse, what is this you've brought me?!" The mouse replied, "This is a gold coin for you, dear stonecutter, perhaps you could use some of it to buy a little meat for me." Touched by her gesture, the stonecutter used a small portion of the gold to buy a sizeable chunk of meat for the mouse.

Their routine continued this way, the mouse delivering gold and the stonecutter providing meat in return, until one unfortunate day when a cat caught the mouse. After persuading the cat not to eat her, she struck a deal to share her daily meat supply in return for her life. As fate would have it, she ended up making the same bargain with two more cats, dividing the meat into smaller portions until she was left with nearly nothing. Consequently, the mouse grew frail and weak.

The stonecutter, worried about her condition, asked, "Mother, what has happened to you? You look unwell." Tired and weak, the mouse revealed her predicament to him. The stonecutter comforted her, saying, "Mother Mouse, you should have told me earlier. I can help you."

The stonecutter chiseled a large crystal block until it became a transparent chamber. He placed the weak mouse inside the chamber in her house, and arranged the crystal block so it would appear as if there was nothing surrounding the mouse. He then advised the mouse to insult the cats when they arrived for their meal.

One by one, the cats came, expecting their share of meat. Each time, the mouse insulted them, and in response, they lunged at her, only to meet the hard, invisible crystal. Each encounter left the cats terrified and believing in the supernatural powers of the mouse, and they never returned.

Once the cats were gone, the stonecutter took Mother Mouse out of the crystal chamber. Out of gratitude, she revealed the hidden gold to the young man. In awe, the stonecutter took the gold and the mouse to his home where they lived in harmony, prosperity, and happiness for the rest of their days.

What to Learn From This Story:

1. **Generosity and kindness can result in unexpected rewards**: The mouse's act of sharing the gold with the stonecutter and feeding the cats despite her predicament showcases her kindness and selflessness. In the end, the stonecutter helps her out of her troubling situation, proving that her initial generosity paid off.

2. **Cunning and intelligence can be stronger than brute force**: Despite being physically weaker than the cats, the mouse managed to outwit them using her intelligence and the stonecutter's crystal trap. This illustrates that brainpower can sometimes be more effective than physical strength.

3. **Never exploit someone's kindness**: The cats took advantage of the mouse's generosity without considering her wellbeing. They ended up scared and humiliated, showing that exploiting others' kindness can lead to negative consequences.

4. **Importance of friendship and compassion**: The bond between the mouse and the stonecutter illustrates the value of friendship and compassion. Their mutual assistance and respect for each other led to a better life for both.

5. **Beware of short-term gains over long-term well-being**: The cats were initially satisfied with the daily meat they received from the mouse, but this short-term gain ultimately led to their humiliation and loss. They might have been better off in the long term had they considered the mouse's welfare instead of just their immediate needs.

The Clever Monkey And The Deceitful Crocodile

In a lush jungle located south of Varanasi, lived a clever and charming monkey. His home was situated near a picturesque stretch of a river where, in the heart of the river, an island abundant with the most delectable fruit trees was found. The monkey made a daily ritual of crossing to the island by leaping onto a lone rock in the river, followed by another jump to the fruit-laden paradise. He usually embarked on his fruit-seeking adventure in the mornings and returned by dusk.

Sharing this stretch of river were a pair of crocodiles. The female crocodile had watched the monkey's routine with growing interest and hunger. Eventually, she craved to feast on the agile and robust monkey and incessantly implored her partner to fulfill her request. After persistent coaxing, he reluctantly vowed to carry out her wish.

His strategy was simple: replace the rock that the monkey routinely used as a stepping stone with his enormous head and lay in wait for the unsuspecting monkey to leap right into his jaws. To perfect his deception, he chose to execute his plan in the evening when the dying light and the growing shadows would mask his true identity.

The monkey, after enjoying a day feasting on the island, prepared for his return journey just as the sun started to set. But as he was about to jump onto the rock, he noticed a peculiar change - the rock appeared unusually high in the water. With the river level remaining unchanged, the monkey sensed something was amiss. To confirm his suspicion, he called out, "Dear Mr. Rock, how do you fare this evening?" The crocodile maintained silence. Undeterred, the monkey continued, "Oh, dear friend, Mr. Rock, why is it that you remain silent tonight?"

The crocodile thought, "If the monkey is accustomed to the rock replying, I must do the same." So, he said aloud, "Good evening, my dear monkey friend, how are you this fine evening?"

"I am doing splendidly," replied the monkey, his suspicions confirmed, "but you, my friend, are certainly not a rock. Who might you be and what do you want?"

"I am a crocodile," admitted the

camouflaged crocodile, "and I have been commanded by my wife to capture you for our evening meal."

The monkey, displaying his quick wit, responded, "Well, since it seems I have no other choice, I must surrender myself to you. Please open your mouth wide and I will jump right in."

The monkey was aware of a peculiar trait of crocodiles - they had to shut their eyes while opening their mouths, rendering them temporarily blind. Seizing this opportunity, he leapt not into the awaiting jaws, but onto the back of the crocodile's head, swiftly following it with another leap to safety on the river bank.

Turning to the disoriented crocodile, the monkey cheerfully said, "It appears your wife will have to settle for another dinner tonight." And off he went. The crestfallen crocodile trudged back to his home, not looking forward to explaining his failure to fulfill his promise to his mate.

What to Learn From This Story:

1. **Cleverness and Quick Thinking**: The story highlights the importance of quick thinking and cleverness in the face of danger. The monkey used his wits to discern the unusual situation and escape from the crocodile's trap. This teaches us to use our intelligence and presence of mind during difficult situations.

2. **Observation and Awareness**: The monkey was able to notice that something was amiss because he was observant and aware of his environment. This shows the value of being observant and paying attention to the details around us, as they can often help us detect potential problems or dangers.

3. **Deception and Trust**: The story also illustrates how deception can lead to failure and loss of trust. The crocodile tried to deceive the monkey but ended up failing in his plan. This shows the negative consequences of dishonesty and teaches us the importance of honesty and trust.

4. **Knowledge and Understanding**:

The monkey was aware of the crocodile's characteristics (closing eyes when opening the mouth) which helped him trick the crocodile. This underlines the importance of knowledge and understanding of one's circumstances, allies and adversaries.

5. **Resilience**: Despite facing a life-threatening situation, the monkey didn't lose hope but instead found a way to overcome the danger. This demonstrates the importance of resilience and determination in overcoming challenges and adversity.

The Monkey And The Peas

Once upon a time, within the royal stables of the magnificent city of Varanasi, resided a monkey. His home was in a tree overlooking a trough used to feed the king's treasured steeds. One sunny day, the trough was brimming with steamed peas, a delight the monkey was particularly fond of. Swiftly, he darted down the tree, his mouth and hands filled to the brim with peas, before he hustled back up to his perch.

As he savored his feast, a single pea slipped from his grip and plummeted to the ground below. Consumed by the loss, the monkey hastily scampered down the tree, dropping the remaining peas in his frenzy. He searched high and low for the missing pea, but to no avail. By the time he admitted defeat, the horses had devoured not only the peas in the trough but also the ones he had unwittingly littered on the ground. Dejected, the monkey climbed back up the tree, his face the picture of gloom.

The stable hands who had been observing the spectacle burst into laughter at the monkey's unfortunate predicament. The king and his most trusted adviser, who had arrived to inspect the horses, also witnessed the sorry state of the monkey. Intrigued, the king turned to his adviser, asking, "My loyal companion, what lesson do you glean from this sight?"

The adviser replied sagely, "Your Highness, such scenarios are commonplace. How often have men forfeited a thousand coins in a futile attempt to reclaim one? How many rulers have sacrificed entire kingdoms for matters of insignificant value?"

Nodding in agreement, the king observed, "Indeed, you speak the truth. Folly is not exclusive to monkeys. It is equally prevalent among humans, regardless of their status—be it a peasant or a king."

What to Learn From This Story:

1. **Value Perspective:** The monkey overvalued a single lost pea while overlooking the abundance it still had in its possession. It's essential to maintain perspective and not let minor setbacks overshadow significant blessings or assets.

2. **Wisdom in Decision Making:**

Reacting impulsively, the monkey rushed to recover the lost pea, which resulted in losing all it had. The story highlights the importance of making thoughtful and wise decisions instead of acting hastily.

3. **Prioritizing Wisely:** The monkey prioritized a single pea over a handful of them. The story serves as a reminder to prioritize wisely, focusing on what's more important or valuable in the long run.

4. **Universality of Folly:** The king's observation at the end suggests that folly is a universal trait, not confined to a particular species or status. It encourages introspection and learning from mistakes, whether they are made by oneself or observed in others.

The River-Dwelling Otters And The Clever Jackal

Once upon a time, nestled amongst the myriad tributaries of the majestic Ganges in the northeastern realms of India, were two otters. These creatures led a lively existence, engaging in hunts, frolicking in the water, and basking in the sun. Not far from their watery abode, a pair of jackals made their den, surviving by foraging along the river for any edible scraps.

On a splendid summer's day, an otter was out hunting in the river when he snagged a magnificent rohita fish. The fish was so enormous that it began to swim away with the otter. Fortunately, he was able to call his partner for assistance, and together they managed to secure their hefty prey. Their initial reaction was exhaustion, but as they regained their breath, they began debating over the division of the massive fish. What started as a discussion soon escalated into a dispute, making it clear that an agreement was not in sight.

At this opportune moment, a male jackal sauntered along the riverbank in search of food. The otters, delighted by his arrival, appealed to him, "Honorable Jackal, could you assist us in resolving this dispute? We can't seem to decide on how to portion this grand fish amongst ourselves."

Assuming an air of authority, the jackal replied in a solemn voice, "I am indeed the right choice for such a matter. I have experience in dealing with many similar predicaments and have always managed to resolve them amicably."

After inquiring about the incident surrounding the fish's capture and examining the fish meticulously, the jackal abruptly instructed, "The head is for you," to the otter on his left, and "The tail, for you," to the otter on his right. Both otters obeyed the jackal's directives and awaited further division.

Then, with an air of finality, the jackal announced, "I shall take the middle as my fee for mediating this dispute." Swiftly, he seized the large middle part of the fish and darted away.

The duped otters stood there dumbfounded, one holding the head, and the other, the tail. The one with the tail let it drop, lamenting, "If we hadn't been so greedy, we would still be enjoying that fine feast."

The other otter, dropping the fish head, responded, "It's a lesson I will remember for a long time to come."

Meanwhile, the jackal delightedly brought the massive piece of fish to his den, much to the delight of his waiting mate.

What to Learn From This Story:

1. **The Consequence of Greed**: The otters' inability to fairly split the fish led them to lose it entirely. Their greed led to their downfall, showing that excessive desire for more can ultimately result in having less or even nothing.
2. **The Importance of Fair Negotiation**: The otters, instead of finding a solution themselves, asked the jackal for help, who took advantage of their disagreement. The story emphasizes the importance of resolving disputes through fair negotiation.
3. **Wisdom Over Deception**: The jackal outsmarted the otters by deceiving them, showing that sometimes, intelligence and cunning can overcome physical power. However, this should also serve as a caution against those who might use

their wisdom for deception.

4. **Learn From Mistakes**: The otters acknowledged their mistake and expressed their determination to learn from it, suggesting the importance of self-reflection and the ability to learn from one's mistakes.

5. **Beware of Those Who Offer to Help for Their Own Benefit**: The jackal had his own interests in mind when he offered to help the otters. The story reminds us to be wary of those who seem to be helping but may be serving their own interests.

The Saga Of The Parakeets And The Prankish Monkey

Many years ago, in the verdant woods skirting the ancient city of Varanasi, dwelled a pair of striking parakeet siblings. The elder of the two was renowned for his profound wisdom, while his younger brother was a fledgling in the ways of the world. Both of them were blessed with dazzling plumage and perfectly sculpted physiques that commanded admiration.

A local trapper, upon witnessing their radiant beauty, hatched a plan to capture and offer them as gifts to the city's monarch. After several attempts, his perseverance bore fruit, and he successfully ensnared the splendid parakeets.

Upon receiving the magnificent birds, the king was overwhelmed with joy, rewarding the trapper handsomely. He ordered the construction of a gilded cage for his new companions, spoiling them with the finest grains, honey, and sugar water served in silver bowls. His frequent interactions with the parakeets soon made them the beloved pets of the entire royal court.

However, the parakeets' golden days were destined to fade. A woodsman, inspired by the bounty the king showered on the trapper, decided to present a large, tamed black monkey to the king. The arrival of the monkey, with its amusing faces and playful antics, quickly shifted the court's attention from the parakeets to their new entertainer. The monkey was pampered with delectable foods and a bed of silk cushions, while the parakeets were pushed into the background, with their meals now composed of common grains and plain water.

Disheartened by their fallen status, the younger parakeet proposed escaping back to the forest. "We deserve better than this! We were the royal favorites, not this monkey!" he complained to his older sibling. The wise elder, however, responded, "We must remember that gain and loss, praise and blame, pleasure and pain, and fame and dishonor are all ephemeral. They all come and go. Just as our fortune shifted, so will the monkey's."

As predicted, the monkey, growing restless and bored in the court, began terrorizing the royal children, pulling faces, flapping his ears and revealing his sharp teeth in a menacing manner. His actions, although amusing to him, terrified the children, causing them to avoid the room where the monkey resided. After their complaints reached the king, he, in a fit of anger, banished the monkey deep into the forest.

With the monkey gone, the court's favor returned to the parakeets. They were once again provided their luxurious foods and were frequently interacted with. Overjoyed by their regained popularity, the younger parakeet said to his elder, "Look, we have regained our rightful place at court and are receiving the attention we deserve." The older parakeet, ever unchanging in his demeanor through good times and bad, merely smiled at his younger sibling and remarked, "Relish these moments, for they too will change."

What to Learn From This Story:

1. **Impermanence**: The story serves as a reminder that everything in life is impermanent. Fortunes rise and fall, and circumstances are ever-changing. The parakeets' time in favor, followed by the monkey's ascension and subsequent fall, illustrates this cyclical nature of life. The elder parakeet understands this, while the younger one learns it

through experience.

2. **Wisdom and Maturity**: The older parakeet displays a depth of wisdom and maturity, understanding the transient nature of their situation. He is not swayed by either the highs of being the court favorite or the lows of being forgotten. This is a valuable lesson in not letting external circumstances impact one's peace of mind.

3. **Deserving Attention**: The younger parakeet's initial reaction to their change in fortune reveals a common misconception that attention or fame is a measure of worth. The story underlines that this is not true and that self-worth should not depend on external validation.

4. **Consequences of Actions**: The monkey's behavior towards the children led to his downfall. This teaches us that our actions have consequences and that being mindful of how we treat others is essential.

5. **Patience and Persistence**: The parakeets' return to favor illustrates the importance of patience and persistence, even in times of difficulty. They endured the harsh phase, and

eventually, things got better.

In sum, the story underscores the importance of wisdom, understanding the nature of life's impermanence, and treating others with respect and kindness.

The Lotus and the Hummingbird

In the heart of a lush forest, where the trees reached the sky and animals thrived, was a serene pond with crystal clear water. In the center of the pond floated a lotus flower, regal and pure, its petals delicately dancing in the breeze. A hummingbird, with iridescent feathers, frequented this secluded spot, attracted by the serene beauty of the lotus.

One day, the hummingbird fluttered towards the lotus, it's wings beating in a blur. "Oh magnificent Lotus, it seems to me, we lead opposite lives. You live in stillness, floating effortlessly, while I'm in constant motion, tirelessly flapping my wings to survive. Yet, we are both vibrant presences in this world. How do you maintain your calm amidst the chaos?" it asked.

The lotus, its petals shimmering under the glistening sun, answered gently, "Dear Hummingbird, our differences stem from our perception and approach towards life. I bloom from the depths of the muddy water, rise above it, and rest in tranquility, embracing the present. You, on the other hand, fly from one flower to another in your quest for nectar, living in a flurry of constant motion."

What to Learn From This Story:

The tale of the hummingbird and the lotus presents significant lessons in mindfulness, gratitude, and happiness.

Mindfulness is being present in the moment, perceiving our surroundings and experiences with attention and acceptance. The lotus, firmly rooted in its environment, teaches us this. Despite the muddy water around it, the lotus chooses to focus on the present, rising above the water surface, and blooming in response to the warmth of the sun. Similarly, we can learn to navigate life's complexities by anchoring ourselves in the present, addressing each situation mindfully, and focusing on our personal growth.

The story also embodies gratitude. The lotus acknowledges its muddy surroundings as a source of nourishment that fuels its growth, rather than an obstacle. It's a gentle reminder for us to express gratitude for our life circumstances, no matter how challenging they may be. By appreciating our experiences and what they teach us, we can turn adversities into opportunities for growth.

Lastly, the tale highlights the pursuit of happiness. Despite their contrasting lifestyles, both the lotus and the hummingbird radiate beauty and vitality in their unique ways. This mirrors our quest for happiness. True happiness does not stem from the external hustle and bustle but from inner peace and contentment. Like the lotus, we must learn to derive happiness from our being and personal growth rather than external validation. Like the hummingbird, we must appreciate the energy of our endeavors and savor the sweet nectar of our efforts.

The Chatty Turtle

Once upon a time, nestled in the foot of the Himalayas, a spectacular lake sparkled under the sun. Two young geese resided here, their lives adorned with the splendor of water lilies and lotus blossoms. The sweet songs of birds from trees along the shoreline were their melodies. On a picturesque stone by the lake, they chanced upon a tortoise, a creature unusually verbose. The tortoise had an innate knack for chatter, seemingly relishing the hours spent conversing with the geese. Despite this, the geese cherished his company, finding his kindness and gentleness irresistible.

The trio enjoyed an idyllic friendship, basking in the warmth of summer and the colors of fall. But winter approached, the season that beckoned the geese to their winter home. The thought of leaving their friend filled their hearts with melancholy.

The tortoise suggested, "I could walk, but by the time I arrive, it might be time for you to return, and then I would..."

"Yes, yes," the geese cut him short, realizing the impracticality of the idea.

After a lot of pondering, an innovative idea struck the geese. They asked the tortoise, "Dear Tortoise, is it true that once your kind bites down on something, nothing can force you to release your grip?"

"Absolutely," the tortoise affirmed, "Our jaws are as strong as iron traps. We can..."

The geese, interrupting his enthusiastic response, laid out their plan. They proposed to hold a sturdy stick at both ends in their beaks. The tortoise could then bite down on the stick, and they could transport him to their winter abode. The only condition was that the tortoise couldn't utter a word during the journey, lest he lose his grip and plummet.

Excited by the prospect, the tortoise agreed eagerly, chattering about his impending aerial adventure. With a firm bite on the stick and the geese lifting him, the journey commenced smoothly. However, they flew lower than usual due to the tortoise's weight.

As they passed over a village, the sight of a turtle being airlifted by geese caught the villagers by surprise. A child yelled, "Hey Tortoise, why are you being carried by those geese?"

Unable to contain his excitement and forgetting the rule, the tortoise yelled back, "These are my friends, they're taking me to their winter home!" The moment the words left his mouth, he lost his grip and plummeted to the ground.

Devastated, the geese circled back, hoping against hope that their friend had survived the fall. But their fears were realized as they found him lifeless, his shell broken from the fall.

Blaming himself, one goose tearfully confessed, "It was my suggestion. Had we not thought of this plan, he would have been safe at the lake."

However, the other goose consoled, "Don't burden yourself with guilt. He knew what was expected of him. His inability to stop talking was his downfall."

What to Learn From This Story:

1. **Importance of Self-Control**: The tortoise's inability to control his chatter led to his downfall. It's essential to exercise self-control, particularly when it's crucial to our well-being or survival.

2. **Consider the Consequences**: The tortoise didn't consider the consequences of breaking the rule of staying silent during the journey. We should always be aware of the potential outcomes of our actions.

3. **Respect for Others' Suggestions**: The geese gave the tortoise clear instructions for their plan to work, but he didn't heed them. It highlights the importance of respecting and following advice or rules laid out by others, particularly when they're for our benefit.

4. **Creativity and Innovation**: The plan created by the geese to help the tortoise migrate with them shows their creativity and problem-solving skills. It teaches us that innovative solutions can often help overcome difficult problems.

5. **Friendship and Trust**: The geese and tortoise shared a strong bond of friendship. They trusted each other, and the geese even devised a plan to stay together. Their friendship, trust, and efforts to help each other demonstrate the power and value of good relationships.

The Partridge, The Primate, And The Mighty Elephant

Once upon a time, nestled in the shadow of the majestic Himalayan peaks, an enormous banyan tree spread its branches. This grand tree was the regular gathering spot for an unusual trio of friends: a partridge, a monkey, and an elephant. Their friendship had been firm since the earliest memories they could muster, but lately, their bond was marred by increasing quarrels and discord. Wishing to preserve their longstanding camaraderie, they concluded that their relationship required a touch of organization. They resolved to establish a hierarchy, designating the eldest among them as their leader, thus aligning their friendship with the established customs of the world.

The mammoth banyan tree was selected as the measure to ascertain the oldest of the three friends.

The partridge turned to the elephant and inquired, "How big was this banyan tree when you first laid eyes on it?"

Deep in thought, the elephant eventually replied, "As a young calf, I recall the banyan tree was nothing more than a seedling, just tall enough to brush against my belly as I lumbered over it."

The monkey was asked the same question, to which he promptly responded, "My dear companions, I distinctly remember as a baby, sitting on the forest floor, I would stretch out and nibble on the tender sprouts of the banyan tree, then a mere shrub."

The question was then put to the partridge. "My memory of this grand tree stretches even further back," answered the bird, a note of nostalgia lacing her voice, "There once stood another majestic banyan tree across the river. I had feasted on its fruit and carried its seeds here in my belly. This magnificent tree that stands before us sprung from those very seeds."

With their jaws dropped in awe, the monkey and the elephant readily acknowledged that the partridge was undoubtedly the eldest of their group and that the position of honor should naturally be hers. They agreed henceforth to pay her due respect and heed her wisdom. The partridge, serious about her newly accorded status, mandated that mutual respect and dignity should govern their behavior, thereby eliminating the roots of their quarrels and ensuring the preservation of their friendship for the rest of their lives.

What to Learn From This Story:

1. **Respect and Honor:** The animals' agreement to respect the partridge due to her age teaches the importance of showing honor and respect to those who are older or more experienced. This lesson is a universal one, applicable in many cultures and societies where elders are revered for their wisdom and experience.

2. **Conflict Resolution:** The friends were able to resolve their disagreements by agreeing to a system of hierarchy. This demonstrates that conflicts, even among close friends, can be effectively resolved by clear communication and agreement on a resolution method.

3. **Mutual Respect and Dignity:** The partridge's decision to ensure all the

animals treat each other with respect emphasizes the importance of treating others with dignity and respect, regardless of their status or position. This is a fundamental principle for maintaining harmony in any relationship.

4. **Acknowledging Differences:** The story also teaches the lesson that differences, such as age in this case, can exist in any group. It's crucial to acknowledge these differences and use them as a basis for understanding and collaboration, rather than discord and disagreement.

The Scarlet Primate And The Ebony Primate

Once upon a time, there was a lush forest on the outskirts of the grand city of Varanasi. The forest was subjected to bouts of heavy rainfall that could last a week. During one such relentless rainstorm, a seasoned ebony primate, soaked to the skin, was trudging through the forest, seeking a refuge from the storm. After an exhaustive search, he chanced upon a comfortable cave shielded by rocks, with a young scarlet primate sitting leisurely at the entrance.

He contemplated, "This young primate will assuredly welcome an elder to share his warm shelter." He stood patiently at the cave entrance, awaiting an invitation that never came. The young primate appeared to be oblivious to his presence.

Indignant, the old monkey thought, "If this youngster will not welcome me, I must resort to trickery." He distended his belly as if he had indulged in a hearty meal and proclaimed, "Ah, those were undoubtedly the most delectable ripe figs I have ever savored, so succulent and sweet."

The scarlet primate was immediately captivated by the mention of ripe figs and said,

"Greetings Uncle, how do you fare? You mention ripe figs. Are they located far from here?"

"Not at all," the ebony primate lied. "I'll provide you with directions, and you'll reach them promptly." Enticed by the promise of juicy figs, the red monkey scampered off, and the old monkey comfortably ensconced himself within the cave.

After a while, the red monkey returned, drenched and disheartened. He had scoured the directed area but didn't find a single fig. The rain showed no signs of relenting, and he was soaked and cold. To his dismay, he found the ebony primate sitting cozily at the cave's entrance.

Grasping that he had been duped, the red monkey decided to give the older monkey a taste of his own medicine. He patted his belly and said, "It was my pleasure to offer my shelter to my respected elder, and your advice was impeccable, Uncle. I've never tasted such delightful figs. There are still plenty left for you."

The ebony primate didn't budge, stared

fixedly at the young primate, and retorted, "Did you show me respect by disregarding my presence in the rain? Only a dim-witted monkey would fall for his own ploy. Be gone, and learn to show appropriate respect to your elders in the future."

Chastened and still dripping, the scarlet primate slunk away to find another shelter.

What to Learn From This Story:

1. **Respect for Elders**: The story highlights the importance of showing respect to elders. When the red monkey failed to invite the elder monkey into the shelter, he behaved disrespectfully. The story thus reminds us that we should always respect and be courteous to our elders.
2. **Consequences of Deceit**: The black monkey used deceit to gain access to the cave, and the red monkey tried to use the same strategy to reclaim his shelter. Neither of their deceitful actions led to a positive outcome, illustrating the point that dishonesty and trickery often backfire.

3. **Learning from Experience**: The black monkey didn't fall for the same trick he played on the red monkey because of his experience. This underscores the value of learning from one's experiences to avoid making the same mistakes again.
4. **Compassion and Sharing**: The red monkey, despite having enough shelter, did not share it with the black monkey initially. The story emphasises the importance of sharing, especially in times of need.
5. **Humility**: In the end, the red monkey learns a lesson in humility when the black monkey sends him away. Pride can often lead to our downfall, so it's essential to remain humble.
6. **Wisdom over Youth**: The story also suggests that wisdom often comes with age and experience. The older black monkey was able to outsmart the younger red monkey due to his wisdom and life experiences.

The Trio Of Aquatic Dwellers

Once upon a time, in the shadow of the majestic Himalayan Mountains, the turbulent waters of the Ganges River were home to three unique fish. The first one was known as Ponderous, who was notorious for overthinking every situation to the point of inaction. The second was named Impetuous, marked by his impulsive nature and lack of forethought. The third fish was Wise, always carefully assessing his surroundings and making decisions judiciously.

These aquatic companions were making their way downstream, feasting on the increasingly abundant food supplies. Yet Wise, aware of the lurking dangers downstream where fishermen laid their traps, voiced his concerns to Ponderous and Impetuous. He suggested, "We ought to return upstream before we become dinner for some humans."

However, Impetuous, entranced by the plentiful food supply, continued his reckless journey downstream, not sparing a second thought to Wise's warning. Ponderous, as usual, found himself ensnared in the trap of indecision, ultimately deciding to trail behind Impetuous. Concerned for his friends, Wise reluctantly followed them but kept a cautious distance.

As feared, Impetuous and Ponderous ended up tangled in a fisherman's net downstream. Witnessing this from afar, Wise knew he had to act swiftly. He made a dash towards the net, splashing vehemently as if he had broken through the net and escaped upstream. Then he swiftly swam to the other end of the net, repeating the same spectacle to create the illusion of a downstream escape. Fooled by Wise's tactics, the fishermen assumed their net was damaged and hastily reeled it in, unwittingly setting Ponderous and Impetuous free.

The near-death experience was a wake-up call for the two wayward fish. Finally understanding the value of Wise's advice, they followed him upstream. Even though the food was less abundant there, they were safe from the predatory humans and their traps.

What to Learn From This Story:

1. **Consideration and Prudence**: The thoughtful fish not only understood the potential dangers that lay ahead but also devised a smart plan to save his friends. This emphasizes the importance of evaluating potential risks before proceeding with a decision.
2. **Consequences of Impulsivity**: The impulsive fish did not consider the possible dangers and blindly rushed ahead because of the immediate rewards (more food). This action nearly cost him his life, teaching us the importance of not being guided solely by immediate gratification.
3. **Paralysis by Analysis**: Overthinking can lead to indecisiveness and failure to act, as shown by the over-thinker fish. It is crucial to strike a balance between thought and action.
4. **Value of Good Advice**: The story underscores the importance of heeding good advice. The impulsive and over-thinker fish initially disregarded the thoughtful fish's advice, leading them into danger.
5. **Importance of Teamwork and Loyalty**: Even though he knew the dangers, the thoughtful fish still

followed his friends, demonstrating the importance of loyalty and teamwork. His quick thinking and actions eventually saved them all.

The Fickle Wolf

Once upon a time, near the mighty Ganges River, a wolf resided on a high, stony ledge along the riverbank. One winter night, while he slumbered, the river flooded, and he awoke to find himself trapped on an island in the river, with perilous currents swirling swiftly around him.

Marooned and foodless, he pondered, "Perhaps there's a silver lining in this predicament. I have no sustenance and absolutely no diversions. Ah! An idea strikes me," he voiced with a newfound enthusiasm, "I shall undertake a sacred fast. I've always been a self-indulgent wolf, primarily concerned with my own needs. Now, I have the opportunity and circumstances to fast, meditate, and contemplate how to evolve into a more virtuous and sacred being. I hereby swear not to eat until the river recedes."

After making the pledge, the wolf adopted the lotus position that he had observed holy men using, appearing genuinely committed to his resolution. To his astonishment, a chubby little goat was swept onto his tiny rocky island soon after.

Upon sighting the goat, the wolf declared,

"I'll commence my fast tomorrow," and lunged at the little goat. However, the goat was remarkably swift and deftly dodged the wolf's attacks every time. Despite repeated attempts, the wolf was always a whisker away from catching the nimble creature. Eventually, utterly spent, he abandoned the chase and returned to his meditation spot. Once he had regained his breath, he announced, "Well, I didn't breach my fast and I shall resume my sacred practices."

Not too far from the island, a large white pelican was swimming and had observed the wolf's spiritual initiation, temporary lapse, and subsequent recommitment. Unable to bear the wolf's duplicity, she swam closer to the island and remarked, "Mr. Wolf, you're truly an extraordinary creature. You take a vow, disregard the vow, and then behave as though the vow was never violated. Vows are as challenging to adhere to as they are simple to declare. A sacred wolf indeed!"

What to Learn From This Story

1. **Integrity and Sincerity**: Your words and actions should align. The wolf makes a vow of fasting, but the moment

food is available, he abandons his commitment. It is essential to uphold our promises, showing integrity and sincerity in our actions.

2. **Consistency and Discipline**: Fasting or self-improvement isn't an easy task, and consistency is key to achieve our goals. The wolf quickly gives up on his vow at the first sight of an easy opportunity, indicating a lack of discipline.

3. **Impulsiveness and Short-Term Gratification**: The wolf's decision to break his fast for immediate gratification underlines the problems of impulsiveness and lack of foresight. It is crucial to resist short-term temptations for long-term benefits.

4. **Accountability**: It's important to hold oneself accountable for one's actions. Instead of acknowledging his failure to stick to his vow, the wolf acts as though nothing happened, demonstrating a lack of accountability.

5. **Authenticity**: Genuine change comes from within and not from external circumstances. The wolf's decision to fast was more out of necessity rather than an inner desire to change, which is

why he could not stick to it when presented with the opportunity to eat.

In conclusion, the story underscores the importance of sincerity, discipline, accountability, foresight, and authenticity.

The Twin Fawns

Once upon a time in the verdant forests to the north of the majestic city of Varanasi, a herd of deer was led by an aged, wise stag. This seasoned deer was an esteemed mentor to many younger ones, who would come under his guidance to understand the subtleties of the forest and the art of survival. One fine day, the elder stag's youngest sister approached him with her twin fawns, saying, "Esteemed brother, my fawns are now at an age where they must understand the secrets of the forest and learn the principles of survival. Would you kindly enlighten them?"

"With pleasure, dear sister. Ask them to join me at noon tomorrow," replied the elder stag.

The following day, as the sun reached its zenith, one of the fawns presented himself for the lessons, while the other was absent. The missing fawn was known for his frivolity and saw more appeal in frolicking in the forest than in the wise words of his elder.

Days turned into weeks with the pattern unchanging; the foolish fawn kept choosing play over knowledge. Then, fate had its way. The frivolous fawn, engrossed in his play, was caught in a hunter's trap. His struggles only tightened the snare, wounding him severely. When the hunter finally arrived, he found the terrified fawn trapped and eventually killed him for his meat.

News of the mishap reached the herd, leaving the mother and the wise elder stag devastated. Despite the loss, the sensible fawn continued his lessons, learning all the wisdom his uncle could impart.

As destiny would have it, the prudent fawn found himself ensnared one day, but his response was distinctly different from his brother's. After alerting the herd of the danger, he started to create an illusion of struggle by digging around the snare. He then feigned death convincingly by puffing his body, rolling his eyes back, and letting his tongue hang out of his mouth, all while suppressing any sign of life.

When the hunter arrived, he was fooled into believing that the fawn had been dead for a while and was starting to rot. He released the snare, intending to butcher the fawn immediately. The moment the hunter turned to retrieve his knives, the clever fawn leaped up and darted into the dense forest, leaving the stunned hunter behind.

What to Learn From This Story

Upon the fawn's return, the herd, especially his mother, was overjoyed. The wise elder stag, though happy, was not surprised; he knew his diligent student had learned his lessons well. The young fawn's return only reinforced the rewards of earnest learning and wisdom.

1. **The importance of education and learning**: The story underlines the crucial role of knowledge and education in survival and navigating through difficulties. The sensible fawn's diligent learning ultimately saves his life.
2. **Wisdom over rashness**: The foolish fawn's rashness and ignorance lead to his unfortunate end, while the wise fawn's thoughtfulness and intelligence ensure his safety. The story emphasizes that wisdom and a calm, measured approach to problem-solving can be life-saving.
3. **The value of listening to elders and experts**: Elders and experts often have a wealth of knowledge and

experience to share. The story shows that ignoring this wisdom can have dire consequences, while taking the time to listen and learn can be beneficial.

4. **The usefulness of cunning and strategy**: The story illustrates how intelligence and strategic thinking can be more powerful than physical strength when facing a challenge. The wise fawn cleverly tricks the hunter, proving that brains can indeed triumph over brawn.

5. **Caution against carelessness and complacency**: The story warns against the dangers of taking unnecessary risks or neglecting serious responsibilities. The foolish fawn's carelessness and nonchalant attitude towards learning important survival skills lead to his demise.

The Deceitful Heron

Once upon a time in the wetlands of northeastern India, there existed a charming little pond, jam-packed with various species of fish. Every year during the severe dry season, the water levels of this pond would dwindle, placing its aquatic inhabitants in grave peril. Observing this predicament, a cunning heron saw an opportunity to satiate his gluttonous desires.

The heron lingered by the pond's edge, pretending to be deep in thought. Noticing this unusual behavior, the leader of the fish swam up to the surface and asked, "Mr. Heron, what is it that occupies your thoughts so deeply, while you abstain from your regular fishing?"

With feigned concern, the heron replied, "Ah, I was pondering over your plight. I fear your home here will soon dry up, and you all will perish. As I was ruminating over this sad fate, it occurred to me that there's a larger, deeper pond not far from here. I would be willing to transport you there, one by one."

Doubtful, the fish retorted, "How do we know you won't just eat us, one by one, if we consent to this plan?"

In response, the sly heron suggested, "If my word isn't enough, allow me to take one of you to the pond and bring you back. That way, you can validate my intentions."

After a council, a brave, one-eyed fish volunteered to be the first to go. True to his word, the heron transported him to the larger pond, which was indeed as luxurious and abundant as promised. Upon returning, the one-eyed fish relayed the amazing prospects of the new home, leading the other fish to consent to the heron's proposal.

With their consent, the wicked heron commenced the transport. Starting with the one-eyed fish, he flew them to a large tree near the bigger pond, devoured them, and discarded their bones at the base of the tree. The cruel cycle continued until the entire fish population was wiped out.

All that remained in the small pond now was a large crab. Approaching him, the heron proposed the same plan. But the crab, suspicious of the heron's bloated appearance, decided to teach the deceitful bird a lesson.

He agreed to the heron's proposal on one condition – he would cling onto the heron's neck with his claws, to ensure he wouldn't be dropped accidentally. The overconfident heron agreed, oblivious to the impending danger.

As they soared over the larger pond, the crab inquired innocently if this was their destination. The heron, now on his dining perch, jeered, revealing his vile intentions. Panicked but determined, the crab tightened his grip around the heron's neck, forcing the bird to descend into the larger pond.

As they touched down, the crab knew his life was at stake the moment he would release the heron. Remembering the fate of his fish friends, he made a swift decision. As the heron leaned in to release him, the crab clamped his powerful claw around the heron's neck, severing it cleanly, just like one would slice a lotus stalk.

Thus ended the reign of the wicked heron, outwitted by the wisdom and bravery of the lone crab.

What to Learn From This Story

1. **Deception and Greed Are Self-Destructive**: The heron's deceptive ways and insatiable greed led to its downfall. Even if one's deceit succeeds in the short term, it will eventually lead to self-destruction.
2. **Wisdom Overcomes Cunning**: The crab, despite being physically weaker than the heron, used his intelligence to defeat the bird. This teaches us that wisdom and clever thinking can help us overcome even the most formidable challenges.
3. **Do Not Easily Trust**: The fish, out of desperation and naivety, trusted the heron without questioning his intentions. This led to their doom. The story thus advises us to be careful about whom we trust, especially during desperate times.
4. **Bravery and Quick Thinking Save the Day**: The crab's courage in confronting the heron and his quick thinking in a crisis saved his life and avenged his friends. The story

underscores the importance of bravery and adaptability in critical situations.

The Strategic Partridge

Once upon a time, nestled in the northeast

of India near the mighty Himalayas, lived an intelligent and vigorous young partridge. Her days were filled with joy as she feasted on seeds and engaged with her fellow birds. She was widely recognized for her sharp wit and judicious demeanor.

However, one day, she overlooked the caution she usually practiced and didn't notice a fowler stealthily approaching her flock while they were absorbed in foraging in a lush meadow. Suddenly, a net cascaded over them, ensnaring a significant number of her companions, including her.

As she writhed, attempting to break free, the hunter carefully bundled up the net, ensuring that no bird could escape. He then started extracting the partridges from the net, one after another, placing them into a sturdy wooden cage. When the hunter reached for our wise partridge, she resisted vehemently, yet she was ultimately unsuccessful in evading capture.

The fowler envisioned selling the birds in the town's market, where they'd be purchased for meals. However, he knew the birds would fetch a higher price if they were plumper than their usual lean physique. He decided to feed them an ample diet of grain and water at his home. The birds, now frantic within the confines of the small cage, fluttered about chaotically, bumping into one another.

Yet, when food was offered, they succumbed to their hunger and indulged — all except for the strategic partridge. She was well-aware of the fowler's scheme and chose to starve herself, growing leaner, and consequently, less appetizing for prospective buyers. This decision meant enduring painful hunger and appearing emaciated, but she realized that this might be her only avenue to freedom.

When the fowler deemed the birds adequately fattened and prepared to take them to the market, he noticed one partridge that was conspicuously thin. He reached into the cage, and the prominent ribcage of the partridge could be felt through her feathers. Puzzled, he took the bird out to investigate her unusual state. The strategic partridge lay motionless until the hunter momentarily loosened his grip.

Seizing this opportunity, she summoned all her remaining strength, freed herself from his grasp, and soared into the sky.

Through her sacrifice and endurance, she managed to secure her freedom. She had endured the pain of hunger and deprivation, but it had allowed her to reclaim her life and the chance to thrive in the coming years. She returned to her remaining flock in the forest and shared her tale of capture and escape, prompting them all to pledge to be more vigilant in watching for hunters in the future.

What to Learn From This Story

1. **Strategic Sacrifice**: The story emphasizes the importance of making sacrifices in the present for the sake of future gains. The partridge chooses to starve and endure hunger, making herself less attractive to potential buyers, which ultimately leads to her escape and survival.

2. **Critical Thinking and Adaptability**: The partridge demonstrates the ability to think

critically about her situation and adapt accordingly. Rather than following the flock's behavior, she assesses the situation, understands the fowler's intentions, and devises a plan to thwart them. This highlights the value of independent thinking and adaptability in dire situations.

3. **Vigilance and Learning from Mistakes**: The partridge and her flock learn a hard lesson about vigilance and the importance of learning from one's mistakes. The oversight that leads to their capture becomes a valuable lesson for the future. They vow to remain alert, preventing a similar situation from happening again.

4. **Courage and Perseverance**: The story portrays the importance of courage and perseverance in the face of adversity. The partridge doesn't give in to fear or despair but instead shows immense courage and determination in her struggle for freedom.

5. **Importance of Strategy over Immediate Gratification**: The partridge's choice to forego immediate gratification (food) for a long-term benefit (freedom) is a valuable lesson.

Often, success and survival require strategy and the ability to delay immediate gratification.

The Hypocritical Dove

Once upon a time, in the northeastern corners of India, lived a grand assembly of doves. The forest, littered with seeds and nuts among fallen leaves and twigs, served as their primary source of sustenance. In the midst of this forest ran a wide road, trodden by numerous wagons carrying a variety of grains and beans destined for the bustling markets of Varanasi. The jostling of these wagons often resulted in the spilling of some grains on the road. The path was also frequented by the elegant carriages of the nobility, drawn by swift horses.

Among the doves, there existed one particularly audacious individual, who relished the delicious morsels scattered on the road while advising her counterparts to steer clear of it. "Dear friends," she would caution, "The road is fraught with dangers. Elephants, ferocious oxen, and swift horses are just some of the hazards that could trample unsuspecting birds." This recurring advice led to her nickname, "The Counselor." However, her appetite for the easy pickings near the road overpowered her own counsel.

One fateful day, while she was indulging in a particularly tasty pile of rice, she noticed a carriage drawing near. She assured herself, "The horse isn't galloping too fast. I surely have time for a few more morsels before taking flight." Alas, her judgment was flawed. The horse, swift as the wind, was upon her before she could react. The wheel of the carriage ran over her, ending her life instantly.

Her sudden disappearance alarmed her flock. After some time, they embarked on a search for her. Overflying the road, a dove spotted the lifeless Counselor lying by the roadside, adjacent to the pile of rice. The shocking sight left him dumbfounded. Despite her constant warnings against the road, there she lay, a casualty of its perils. He swiftly returned to the flock and led them to the tragic sight.

Hovering above their fallen friend, one dove solemnly stated, "Her advice was sound; it's unfortunate she didn't heed it herself. Greed can indeed lead to the most tragic outcomes."

What to Learn From This Story

1. **Hypocrisy**: The story illustrates the negative consequences of hypocrisy. The dove who warned others about the dangers of the road, yet couldn't resist the temptation herself, highlights the importance of practicing what you preach.

2. **Greed**: The dove's greed led her to ignore her own advice, ultimately resulting in her death. This teaches us that excessive greed can blind us to risks and lead to negative outcomes.

3. **Misjudgment**: The dove misjudged the speed of the approaching carriage, which ended up costing her life. This emphasizes the importance of accurate assessment in making decisions.

4. **Consistency between Words and Actions**: The story highlights the importance of aligning our actions with our words. Not doing so can damage our credibility and may lead to unfortunate consequences, as it did for the dove.

5. **Respect for One's Own Advice**: If a piece of advice is worth giving to others, it's worth following oneself.

The story underscores the importance of not only offering sound advice but also adhering to it.

The Hermit And His Forest Friends

In a distant epoch, a wise man, seeking enlightenment, decided to live in solitude amidst the towering peaks of the Himalayas. One particular summer, a devastating drought had gripped the area, causing streams to dry up under the relentless sun. In response to his need for water, the wise hermit dug a well.

The inhabitants of the forest, the animals, were greatly suffering due to the water scarcity, with many at the brink of death. Feeling a profound compassion for these creatures, the hermit resolved to assist them. He cut down a sizable dead tree and carved out its middle to fashion a capacious trough. The task was physically demanding in the unbearable heat, yet he carried on, aware that the animals' survival was at stake. Once the trough was ready, he proceeded to fill it with water from his well, an equally laborious task, but he managed to accomplish it.

The desperate animals of the forest, guided by the scent of the precious liquid, gradually began to approach the trough. Initially, it was the smaller creatures like birds, rabbits, and squirrels that ventured forth. Then, larger animals such as deer and wild boars quenched their thirst. Eventually, even the mighty tiger came, drinking from the hermit's trough in a rare moment of peace.

The hermit had to devote almost all his time to replenishing the water in the trough, so much so that he barely had time to forage for his meals. Seeing his waning strength, the animals decided to repay his kindness. They knew hidden corners in the forest where they could still find edible roots, berries, and fruits. They gathered these for the hermit, who was deeply touched by their reciprocation of his kindness. Throughout the drought, this cycle continued—the hermit providing water for the animals, and the animals bringing food for the hermit.

Finally, when the rains arrived and the drought was no more, the streams filled up again. The hermit no longer needed to maintain the trough, and he could now gather his own food. However, the bond that he had formed with the animals persisted. The animals would often visit, resting near his humble abode or perching on the nearby trees, content in the company of the friend who had once saved their lives.

What to Learn From This Story

1. **Compassion and Kindness:** The hermit's actions demonstrate the importance of compassion and kindness. Regardless of the hardships he faced, he persisted in providing water for the animals during a drought, showcasing his selfless concern for others' wellbeing.
2. **Interconnectedness and Mutual Aid:** The hermit's relationship with the animals embodies the interconnectedness of all life forms. The animals reciprocated the hermit's kindness by providing food for him when he needed it, illustrating the mutual aid and cooperative survival that can exist in nature.
3. **Gratitude and Reciprocity:** The animals' efforts to help the hermit reflects gratitude and the principle of reciprocity. They remembered the hermit's kindness and returned the favor, which indicates the importance of appreciating and repaying kindness whenever possible.
4. **Harmony and Peace:** The peaceful coexistence between the hermit and the animals, even including a tiger,

highlights the possibility of harmony among diverse creatures. It's a testament to the peace that can be achieved when we approach others with kindness and understanding.

5. **Persistence and Resilience:** The hermit's consistent effort to provide water, even in the face of extreme physical hardship, exhibits the virtues of persistence and resilience. It teaches us to continue our good efforts, even when they are challenging.

The Raven And The Elegant Ducks

Once upon a time, in the grand metropolis of Varanasi, there dwelled a raven who survived by being a scavenger, feasting on carcasses and pilfering leftovers left out by humans. He was a crafty bird, always discontented with his lot. In an ambitious quest to diversify his diet, he ventured along the Ganges River, hoping to find any deceased fish washed up on its banks. While scouting, he spotted a pair of magnificent ruddy ducks gliding serenely on the river. Intrigued, he pondered, "How striking these ducks are with their radiant red hue. I wonder what delicacies they consume to possess such dazzling colors. I must find out and consume the same to transform my dull grey and black plumage into that vibrant reddish tone."

With this plan in mind, he swooped down and alighted on the riverbank, approaching the ducks, "Esteemed avian companions, may I inquire what variety of fish or meat you consume to bestow upon your feathers such a splendid color?"

The ducks glanced at the raven warily, well aware of the notorious reputation of these birds. The male duck responded, "Mr.

Raven, we consume neither fish nor any form of flesh. It's against our nature to consume another being's body. Our sole desire is peace and happiness for all. Our diet consists solely of aquatic plants from the river bed. This is sufficient for our sustenance."

"Impossible," retorted the raven, "Aquatic plants cannot possibly yield the vibrant color of your plumage. There must be some secret food you feast upon and are withholding from me. I consume an array of meats and whatever I can scavenge, yet my plumage remains these drab tones."

"Raven," interjected the female duck, "our diet is indeed limited to aquatic plants. However, beauty is not solely determined by what you consume but also by your actions. You are a creature known for theft and feasting on your fellow beings' flesh. Do not anticipate radiating beauty under such conditions. Transform your habits. Prioritize others' wellbeing, and beauty will follow naturally."

Upon hearing this, the raven looked at the ducks disdainfully and retorted, "If that's the secret, I'll forgo your beauty. I'm content with my lifestyle." With a piercing "Caw! Caw! Caw!" echoing through the air, he took flight, resuming his search for deceased fish.

What to Learn From This Story

1. **The Inner Self Reflects on the Outer Appearance**: The story emphasizes the belief that our outer appearance often reflects our inner self. The raven, with its habits of scavenging and theft, maintained a drab appearance, while the peaceful and herbivorous ducks had vibrant and beautiful plumage.

2. **Peace and Kindness Nurture Beauty**: The ducks symbolize peaceful living and kindness to all beings. They illustrate that these qualities bring a kind of beauty that cannot be achieved through superficial means, such as diet alone.

3. **Acceptance and Contentment**: The raven's final reaction shows the importance of acceptance and contentment. Despite the prospect of becoming more beautiful, the raven chooses to accept its nature and

continue its way of life. This implies a sense of contentment with one's nature, despite its flaws.

4. **The Futility of Imitation**: The raven's initial intent was to imitate the ducks' diet to gain their beauty. However, the story points out the futility of such imitation. True change and growth come from within, based on one's actions and intentions, not merely by copying others.

5. **Wisdom Over Appearance**: The ducks' wisdom in their response to the raven illustrates the value of wisdom over mere physical appearance. They knew that their beauty came from their lifestyle and their inner peace, rather than their diet. This places a higher value on wisdom and inner peace than on external beauty.

The Majestic Ruru

A long time ago in a northeastern

kingdom of India, there resided a splendid creature known as the Ruru deer. This magnificent animal had chosen to dwell within the heart of the kingdom's forest, keeping its existence a secret from humans. The deer was an extraordinary sight to behold - its glistening, golden coat dotted with iridescent spots reminiscent of rubies, emeralds, and sapphires. The inviting warmth of its sparkling blue eyes and the gleaming marble-like quality of its horns and hooves contributed to its allure. The Ruru deer was well aware of its allure and knew that its magnificent appearance would incite the greed of men. Being wise, it had learnt to dodge the pitfalls, snares, and traps set by men and had also imparted this knowledge to other forest dwellers to protect them.

Following a severe rainstorm, the Ruru deer was alerted by an unfamiliar noise from the river. Upon reaching the riverbank, it found a man battling the turbulent waters, pleading desperately for assistance. Touched by the man's plight, the deer plunged into the water, battling the vicious currents to reach the struggling man. "Climb onto my back," the deer instructed calmly, "and I'll carry you to safety."

The man, awestruck by the magnificent creature, complied, and together they made it to the riverbank. The Ruru deer tended to the weakened man, providing warmth and guiding him back to his city once he had recovered. Touched by the deer's act of kindness, the man inquired, "You have saved my life and shown me such compassion. How can I repay you?"

"Gratitude," the deer replied, "is a trait that should be instinctive. However, in today's world, it is considered a virtue. I'm pleased to see it in you. My only request is that you never divulge my existence to anyone. If word spreads of my existence, men will never cease their pursuit until they have captured me."

The man agreed to this request, considering it a small price to pay for the deer's kindness.

Meanwhile, the queen of the city, known for her prophetic dreams, dreamt of the magnificent Ruru deer. Overwhelmed by the vision of the resplendent deer sharing its wisdom with the king and his court, she immediately relayed her dream to the king. Given the queen's track record of accurate premonitions, the king sent out his hunters to find this extraordinary creature, promising a handsome reward to the person who succeeded in this quest.

The man saved by the Ruru deer, living in the city and faced with dire poverty, heard of the king's proclamation and the promised reward. The lure of wealth made him contemplate betraying the deer that had saved his life. Torn between gratitude and temptation, he ultimately succumbed to the allure of wealth and led the king and his soldiers to the Ruru deer's dwelling in the forest.

The king's forces encircled the area, drawing the net closer and closer around the Ruru deer. As the king prepared to shoot his arrow at the deer, the Ruru deer asked the king how he had been found. The king revealed that the man beside him, the one who was saved from drowning, was his guide. The deer recognized the man instantly and stated, "An ungrateful man would have been better off left in the river."

Perplexed, the king requested an explanation, and the deer recounted the tale of his rescue of the guide who now stood before them, head bowed in shame. The king, turning to the man, asked if the deer's account was true. The man confirmed the truth of the story, prompting the king to draw his bow towards him, ready to deliver justice for his betrayal.

However, the Ruru deer once again showcased its kindness, stepping between the man and the king's drawn bow, pleading for the man's life. "Please don't harm a man already wounded by his greed. His greed has hurt him as it has hurt many men. Let him live to learn from his mistakes," the deer implored.

Touched by the mercy and wisdom displayed by the deer, the king pardoned the man's life and guaranteed the safety of the Ruru deer throughout his kingdom. In return, the king requested the deer to accompany him back to his court and teach his subjects about mercy and kindness.

In accordance with the queen's dream,

the Ruru deer journeyed to the court, sharing its teachings and wisdom, thus enlightening the king's subjects.

What to Learn From This Story

1. **Gratitude**: The story emphasizes the importance of gratitude. Even though the Ruru deer saved the man's life, the man betrayed the deer for his personal gain, showcasing the dire lack of gratitude.

2. **Wisdom and Kindness**: The Ruru deer's wisdom and kindness are consistently displayed throughout the story, teaching the importance of these virtues. Despite being betrayed, the deer intervenes to save the man's life, teaching that wisdom and kindness should not be compromised regardless of others' actions.

3. **The Dangers of Greed**: The man's betrayal of the deer demonstrates the destructive potential of unchecked greed. His desire for wealth overshadows his gratitude and leads him to betray the one who saved his life.

4. **Learning from Mistakes**: The deer's plea to the king to let the man live and learn from his mistakes underlines the significance of learning from our errors and growing from them.

5. **Mercy and Forgiveness**: The king's decision to spare the man, influenced by the Ruru deer's display of mercy, illustrates the power of mercy and forgiveness.

6. **The Value of Keeping Promises**: The man breaks his promise to the Ruru deer, leading to severe consequences. This teaches us the importance of keeping our word.

7. **The Impact of One's Actions on Others**: The story also shows how our actions can have unforeseen consequences on others, as seen by the peril the Ruru deer faces due to the man's betrayal. It emphasizes the importance of considering the wider impact of our decisions.

The Considerate Ox

Many moons ago, in the fertile lands of

Gandhara, Northwest India, a compassionate farmer lived. This farmer, deeply empathetic to all living creatures, once purchased a young bull calf. He cared for this
young creature like his own child, fostering
a bond akin to father and son. Owing to his
love for the bull, he named him "Bliss ".

As years passed, the calf matured into a
splendid ox, radiating strength from his
muscular frame. Feeling indebted to his
master's kind treatment, Bliss one day suggested, "Dear master, I am confident in my
strength. Why don't you approach a
wealthy merchant, willing to wager a thousand silver pieces that I can haul a hundred
fully laden carts?"

"Bliss," responded the farmer, "it's a substantial wager. Are you certain you can bear
such weight?"

"More than certain," replied Bliss confi-
dently.

Excited by the prospect, the farmer visited the town. He found the merchant with
the most robust oxen and casually

introduced his claim. Disbelieving, the merchant challenged, "An ox hauling such weight is impossible!"

"My farm says otherwise," the farmer replied calmly. "Would you care to wager?"

"A thousand silver pieces that your ox can haul a hundred carts," said the farmer.

"Agreed!" the merchant answered swiftly.

After two days of preparations, everything was ready. The carts were filled and linked at the outskirts of the town. Bliss was bathed, fed scented rice, garlanded with flowers, and yoked to the convoy of carts. The farmer, apprehensive about the massive load and the high stakes, took his seat on the first cart and shouted at Bliss, "You brute! Move these carts, wretch! Pull with all your strength, you devil!"

These insults stung Bliss deeply. "Devil! Wretch! Brute!" He had never faced such harsh words. Feeling insulted and demeaned, his legs refused to budge. Despite the farmer's whipping and further abuse, Bliss did not move an inch. The farmer lost the wager, paid the silver, and retreated to his farmhouse, devastated.

Bliss wandered home and stuck his head through the farmhouse window, asking, "Dear master, are you sleeping?"

"Sleeping? After losing a thousand silver pieces?" the farmer retorted. "Why did you not try to move the carts?"

"Master," Bliss calmly replied, "have I ever been a problem to you? Have I caused harm or shown any malice to you or your family?"

"Never," the farmer admitted.

"Why then," asked Bliss, "did you call me a wretch, a brute, a devil, and strike me with a whip?"

Feeling shame, the farmer confessed, "Bliss, I understand now. I let my greed for wealth and fear of loss overshadow our friendship. I apologize."

Bliss then advised, "Go to the merchant and propose a wager of two thousand silver pieces, under the same conditions. I believe he will accept."

The farmer did as advised, and the merchant agreed, envisioning another easy victory. The townsfolk jeered as Bliss was yoked to the carts, remembering his previous failure. However, this time the farmer, whipless, addressed the ox gently, "Bliss, my dear friend, move the last cart to where the first is now."

With immense effort, Bliss began to move, and the line of carts followed. The last cart eventually reached the position of the first. The farmer collected his winnings amidst thunderous applause from the amazed crowd.

Turning to the spectators, Bliss imparted, "Gentle words can move mountains, while insults only stir hurt and resentment."

What to Learn From This Story

1. **Kindness and Empathy:** The most compelling lesson is the power of kind and empathetic words. They can motivate and inspire action far more effectively than harsh words or force.

2. **Respect:** The farmer initially forgot to respect his ox, treating him like an object rather than a living being. This story shows the importance of treating all creatures with respect.

3. **Greed and Fear:** The farmer's greed for money and fear of loss led him to forget his bond with the ox. This shows how negative emotions can cloud our judgement and lead to poor decisions.

4. **Apology and Redemption:** The farmer recognized his mistake and apologized. This teaches us the value of admitting our mistakes and taking steps to correct them.

5. **Perseverance:** Despite the initial failure, the ox, with the farmer, didn't give up and tried again. This illustrates the value of not giving up even when facing adversity.

6. **Friendship:** The story also emphasizes the depth of the bond

between the farmer and the ox, portraying a beautiful example of friendship between humans and animals.

The Myna Birds And The Flaming Tree

Once upon a time, in the dense greenery just south of the majestic city of Varanasi, a group of myna birds resided within the mighty branches of an ancient pippala tree. This tree had served as their ancestral home for countless generations. During a particular gusty day, the insightful leader of the flock noticed that the friction between two dry, dead branches was producing smoke. Given the arid season and the tree's fill of withered leaves and dried timber, he concluded, "The tree is a tinderbox, awaiting a spark. We are in grave danger."

Swiftly, he spread his wings across the entirety of the tree, alerting his flock, "We must evacuate this tree immediately! It's a ticking time bomb, ready to ignite!" Those birds with a strong sense of prudence heeded his advice without delay, escaping the tree to take refuge in neighboring trees a considerable distance away.

However, among the flock were skeptics. Some dismissed the leader, remarking, "He's just a worrywart, seeing dangers where none exist." Others chimed in with mocking laughter, asserting they had never witnessed a tree spontaneously combusting. But as their ridicule echoed through the branches, the inevitable happened - the tree ignited. The flames erupted rapidly at the source of friction, spreading wildly through the arid woodwork. Gusts of wind carried plumes of thick smoke up into the tree's higher branches. The birds who had chosen to remain found themselves quickly overwhelmed by the smoke and, unable to escape, plummeted into the fiery inferno below.

What to Learn From This Story

From their safe distance, the prudent birds watched in stunned silence as their comrades succumbed to the catastrophic fire, a potent reminder of the deadly cost of dismissive ignorance.

1. **Listen to Warnings:** The leader bird's warning was based on his observations and knowledge. Those birds who ignored it paid a fatal price. When someone who has experience or knowledge issues a warning, it is wise to heed their advice.

2. **The Danger of Complacency:** The birds who dismissed the warnings were complacent and overconfident, assuming that just because they hadn't seen something happen before, it couldn't happen. This underestimation of potential risks can lead to devastating consequences.

3. **The Importance of Quick Action:** In dangerous situations, it is crucial to act promptly. The birds that took immediate action upon hearing the leader's warning were the ones who survived.

4. **Respect for Wisdom and Experience:** The story emphasizes the importance of respecting the wisdom and experience of others. The leader bird, due to his keen observation and understanding, was able to foresee the danger that others could not.

5. **The Consequences of Skepticism:** While healthy skepticism can sometimes be beneficial, in this story, it led to disaster. The skeptic birds doubted the leader's wisdom, leading to their tragic end. This teaches us that unwarranted skepticism, especially in

the face of clear evidence, can be harmful.

The Brother Oxen And The Lavish Pig

In the verdant outskirts of the ancient city of Rajgir, there thrived a rich farmstead where dwelt two oxen siblings. The more matured of the pair was dubbed Big Red and his younger sibling was known as Little Red. The farmstead was lively with the farmer's substantial family, with the eldest daughter's wedding looming on the horizon. Day after day, the oxen diligently tilled the fields and hauled carts brimming with heavy loads. As dusk fell, their reward was a simple fare of grass hay and grain chaff.

One evening, while chewing through their modest meal, Little Red's gaze wandered to the snug sty across the yard. There, a pig named Lotus Root was indulging in a feast of sugary rice porridge and tantalizing scraps from the table. Little Red expressed his dismay, "Beloved brother, why is it that we, toiling tirelessly from dawn to dusk, have but hay and chaff to satiate our hunger, while Lotus Root, who idles her time away, dines on cooked porridge and a variety of delectable dishes?"

Big Red, responding to his brother's concerns, said, "Dear sibling, don't harbor resentment for Lotus Root's extravagant meals. The delight she is relishing now comes at a steep price. The farmer's daughter's wedding is approaching and, when that day arrives, Lotus Root will be sacrificed and her flesh will be minced to prepare the wedding curry. Our honest labor, though it yields simple food, guarantees us a life of longevity."

The wedding day dawned and Big Red's ominous prophecy unfolded to the letter. As the slaughterer's knife descended on Lotus Root, her agonizing screams pierced the air. Little Red, trembling at the horrific sight, turned to Big Red, "Oh sagacious brother, our humble meals are a hundred, no, a thousand times superior to the grand feasts that were the undoing of poor Lotus Root."

What to Learn From This Story

1. **The Value of Hard Work:** The oxen may have a simple life, laboring in the fields and consuming plain food, but their hard work provides them with longevity and safety. They earn their keep and are valued for their consistent contribution.
2. **Avoiding Envy:** It's easy to be envious of others who seem to have a better or easier life. However, as Little

Red discovers, appearances can be deceptive. What may seem like a luxurious life may have its own drawbacks or dangers, as it did for Lotus Root.

3. **Understanding True Prosperity:** Wealth or prosperity isn't always about having the most lavish of meals or an easy life. True prosperity can lie in health, longevity, and the satisfaction derived from honest labor.

4. **Being Content with What One Has:** Big Red shows wisdom in accepting their simple life and understanding the real reason behind Lotus Root's seemingly extravagant lifestyle. This leads to gratitude for what they have rather than yearning for what they don't.

5. **The Consequences of Short-term Pleasure:** Lotus Root's life is filled with pleasure and abundance in the short term, but it leads to a tragic end. The story implies that indulging in short-term pleasures without considering the long-term consequences can lead to regrettable outcomes.

The Clever Strategy Of The Lion And Wild Boar

In the shadowy foothills of the mighty

Himalayas, a ferocious lion resided in a comfortable den. One day, after feasting on a large water buffalo, the lion decided to stop by a lake to quench his thirst on his way back to his abode. At the lake, he spotted a boar sipping water. Given his stuffed belly, the lion had no intention of attacking the boar, but hoping to encounter it again when he might be hungry, he chose not to scare it away and retreated into the bushes.

However, the boar, in its vanity, misinterpreted the lion's actions as fear. It told itself, "This lion is fleeing from me, intimidated by my strength and formidable appearance. Today, I will challenge this cowardly lion!"

The boar shouted out, "Lion, don't flee! Stand and fight like a true warrior. I hold no fear of you."

The lion, taken aback by the audacity of the boar, saw an opportunity. He replied, "Dear friend, I'm unable to accept your challenge today. However, I'm willing to meet you here in one week's time for the duel."

The boar gleefully accepted the terms, returning to its herd and narrating the day's events. "I will vanquish this lion, etching the name of our species into the annals of eternal fame!"

The herd's leader retorted, "You're out of your mind! No boar stands a chance against a lion. You're courting death."

The boar, rattled by these words, started to question its rash decision. "What should I do? If I don't show up, he will hunt me down," the boar agonized. "Indeed," agreed the leader, "and he'll discover the rest of us, leading to numerous casualties. You must attend the duel. But I have a plan. For the next six days, roll in a dunghill, allowing the feces to dry and form a layer over your body each day. On the seventh day, just before the duel, moisten yourself with dew drops to evoke the foulest stench possible. Arrive early at the battleground and position yourself so that the wind blows from your direction."

The boar adhered religiously to the leader's directions. On the day of the duel, it stood by the lake, wrapped in a layer of dung, emanating an unbearably foul stench. The lion, being a creature of cleanliness, was repulsed by the sight and the stink of the boar. His eyes teared up due to the pungent odor, and he told the boar, "I can't even bear to touch you, let alone bite you. You've won this duel, but with the most repugnant strategy I've ever seen." Disgusted, the lion left to find a less distasteful meal.

The boar, bursting with foolish pride, hastily returned to the herd to boast about his unlikely victory.

What to Learn From This Story

1. **Never underestimate your opponent:** The boar initially underestimates the lion, but he quickly realizes that the lion is a formidable opponent.
2. **Strategic thinking can turn the odds in your favor:** Despite being physically outmatched, the boar uses a clever strategy to neutralize the lion's strength and win the challenge.
3. **Not all battles are won by brute force:** Sometimes, unconventional

approaches and smart tactics can defeat a more powerful opponent.

4. **Pride and overconfidence can lead to dangerous situations:** The boar's pride and overconfidence almost lead him into a deadly duel with the lion. It's important to assess one's own capabilities accurately and not to allow vanity to cloud judgment.

5. **Victory attained through distasteful means may not be honorable:** Though the boar wins the duel, the method it uses isn't respectable. It's important to bear in mind the means through which we achieve our goals.

Friends In Need: The Antelope, The Woodpecker, And The Tortoise

Once upon a time, in the forest region to the north of the magnificent city of Varanasi, there thrived a trio of unlikely companions - an antelope, a woodpecker, and a tortoise. They lived by a serene, crystalline lake, each one strikingly different from the other, yet bonded by an endearing friendship that was a testament to their mutual respect and affection.

One fateful day, a hunter stumbled upon the antelope's hoofprints etched by the lakeside. Sensing an opportunity, he meticulously set up a leather snare to ensnare the creature. As dusk drew its blanket over the sky, the antelope arrived at the lake for a drink, oblivious to the trap lying in wait. Caught in the snare, panic gripped him, prompting a distress call.

The woodpecker and tortoise, alarmed by their friend's cry, rushed to his aid. Witnessing the antelope trapped in the snare, they knew his fate would be grim if the hunter found him. Quick thinking and cooperation were necessary. The woodpecker, upon contemplating, turned to the tortoise, "Can you gnaw through those leather straps?"

The tortoise nodded, "I can. But it's a sturdy trap. It would require some time to free our friend."

"Then start gnawing," the woodpecker instructed, "I will try to hold the hunter back."

The following morning, the hunter prepared to check his snares. As he opened the front door, the woodpecker swooped into his face. The hunter, shaken by the encounter, retreated into his hut to recover. Hours later, the hunter attempted to leave again, this time from the back door, only to be startled by the woodpecker once more. The baffled hunter decided to stay put, fearing misfortune.

However, the woodpecker knew he couldn't deter the hunter forever. On the second day, he flew back to the tortoise and the antelope, announcing the imminent arrival of the hunter. The tortoise, despite a sore and bleeding mouth, had almost gnawed through the last strap. With a final effort, he released the antelope, who sprinted away just as the hunter emerged on the scene.

While the woodpecker flew to safety, the spent tortoise lay helpless on the ground. Intrigued by the tortoise's heroic act, the hunter decided to cook him into a soup. He put the tortoise in his sack and was ready to leave when the antelope, who had been watching from the thicket, decided to act.

Feigning a limp, the antelope lured the hunter away from the lake. The hunter, seeing an opportunity to catch the antelope, hung the bag containing the tortoise on a tree and gave chase. Leading the hunter deeper into the forest, the antelope cleverly shook him off and returned to free the tortoise.

Using his sharp horns, the antelope retrieved the bag from the tree, delicately slit it open, and liberated the tortoise. Overwhelmed with gratitude, the antelope said to his friends, "You have shown me the true meaning of friendship today. However, I fear we must relocate our families for safety. Let's hope that we meet again under safer circumstances." And so, the three friends bid their farewells, embarking on separate journeys to new homes, far away from the perils of the hunter.

What to Learn From This Story

1. **The Power of Friendship**: The story underscores the power of true friendship. Despite their stark differences, the antelope, woodpecker, and tortoise worked together to outwit the hunter. They each used their unique abilities to contribute to the common goal of saving each other, highlighting how our differences can be our strength when we cooperate and respect one another.

2. **Courage and Sacrifice**: Both the woodpecker and the tortoise put their lives at risk to help their friend, the antelope. They showed courage and selflessness, reflecting that sometimes, one has to make sacrifices for the sake of friends.

3. **Cleverness and Quick Thinking**: The story demonstrates that cleverness and quick thinking can overcome even the direst situations. The woodpecker's idea to distract the hunter and the antelope's strategy to

lead the hunter away shows the importance of innovative problem-solving.

4. **Adaptability**: At the end of the story, the animals recognize the ongoing threat of the hunter and make the tough decision to move to a new home. This highlights the importance of adaptability in the face of changing circumstances.

5. **Respect for All Life**: The hunter's decision to trap and eat the animals is portrayed negatively, teaching the reader to respect all life forms.

The Brave Monkey Chief

In the lush valleys near the mighty Himalayan Mountains, there was a peepul tree so special that it was like a magical treasure. Its beauty was beyond compare, and when it bloomed in spring, it looked like a giant white cloud floating in the forest. The fruit it bore was incredibly delicious and fragrant.

This extraordinary tree was the home of a troop of monkeys led by a wise and caring king. The monkey king was strong and beloved by all. He always helped and protected his fellow monkeys, no matter how small they were.

The monkeys happily feasted on the peepul tree's fruit, and their king knew how precious it was. He had one important rule: during spring, they must pluck all the blossoms that hung over the nearby Ganges River. If even one fruit fell into the river and was found by humans, it could lead them to the monkeys' home, and that would be disastrous.

One year, the monkeys missed a single

blossom hidden by leaves, and it grew into a fruit. Unfortunately, it fell into the river and drifted downstream to the city of Varanasi, where the king's wives discovered it. The fruit's heavenly scent and taste amazed the king, and he became determined to find its source.

With a troop of soldiers, the king searched for days until they found the peepul tree and its monkeys. Furious that the monkeys were enjoying the delicious fruit he desired, the king ordered his archers to attack. The monkeys were trapped with no escape.

But the monkey king didn't give up. He saw another tree across the river, and he made a daring leap to become a bridge for his troop. He sacrificed his safety to save his beloved monkeys. Once they all crossed to safety, he fell back, wounded and unconscious.

The ruler of Varanasi was moved by the

monkey king's bravery and compassion. He ordered the monkey to be carefully treated and asked, "Why did you risk yourself for others?"

"I am their leader and father figure," said the monkey king. "I had to protect them, no matter the cost."

"But in human kingdoms, the king is served by the people, not the other way around," said the ruler.

"That may be true for men, but compassion guides me. I had to save my troop," said the monkey king.

"But what did you gain from this?" asked the ruler.

"I gained the survival of my troop and showed you how a true king rules with love and compassion," said the monkey king before passing away.

The ruler of Varanasi respected the

monkey king's sacrifice. He arranged a royal cremation and ordered his troops to leave without taking a single fruit. The peepul tree remained the home of the great monkey king's troop.

What to Learn From This Story

1. **Compassion and Sacrifice:** The story teaches us the value of compassion and self-sacrifice. The monkey king's love for his troop led him to risk his life to save them, setting an example of true leadership.

2. **Leading by Example:** The monkey king's actions showed that being a good leader means caring for others and putting their well-being before your own. He demonstrated that true kingship comes from empathy and kindness.

3. **Importance of Community:** The story emphasizes the significance of a close-knit community. The monkey king's troop was like a family, and they supported and protected each other in times of need.

4. **Appreciation for Nature:** The story reminds us to value and protect nature. The peepul tree was a precious resource for the monkeys, and the monkey king was willing to safeguard it for the greater good.

The Scavenger Bird

Long ago in northeast India near a place

called Vulture's Peak, there lived a wise vulture king who ruled a large flock. In doing their job of eating carrion, the vultures helped to keep their region clean and free of disease.

The king had a son who was very strong and large. The son was fortunate to have a wife who adored him and three fine children. With his keen eyesight and sharp sense of smell, which enabled him to detect carrion from a great distance, he was the envy of the flock. But he was admired most of all for his flying abilities. He could fly faster and higher than any other vulture, and he often did. In fact, he flew so high that his friends began to worry about him. They had heard that it was dangerous to fly to such heights and they told the king of their fear.

Concerned about his son's welfare, the king sent for him. "I have heard," said the king, "that you have been flying very high into the sky. Is that true?" The son replied, "Yes, but it is not a danger for me. I am much stronger than my friends and have no difficulty in flying to great heights."

The king said, "We vultures are meant to

fly only so high, and if we go beyond that point we will die. That applies to you as well as to all other vultures. When you are soaring high in the sky and the earth is but a small field in your vision, you have gone as far as you can, and you should go no further."

The son listened respectfully to his father and left, but the next time he was out flying with his friends, he decided to impress them with his highest flight yet. He felt his strength and size made him different from other vultures and he wanted the others to observe his superiority. He caught a strong updraft from the mountains and started soaring higher and higher. Some of his friends were flying with him; they told him he was going too high, and they stopped their own ascent. He laughed at them and said he could go much higher. As he ascended, he could see the earth become only a small field in his vision, as his father had said, but he kept on going. Upward he spiraled until he was completely out of sight from the ground. He felt invincible and went higher and higher. Then in a flash, as if he were struck by a blast of icy wind, he was unconscious. He lost all control of his flight and plummeted to the ground and was killed on impact.

The vulture's friends, father, wife, and children all gathered around his shattered body and wept.

What to Learn From This Story

1. **Listen to Wise Advice**: The vulture's father warned him about the dangers of flying too high, but he didn't heed the advice and faced tragic consequences. It teaches us to listen to wise counsel and not let overconfidence cloud our judgment.
2. **Hubris Can Lead to Disaster**: The vulture's pride and belief in his invincibility led him to take unnecessary risks, resulting in his untimely death. It reminds us to be humble and aware of our limitations.
3. **Respecting Limits**: Each creature, including humans, has its limitations. Understanding and respecting these limits are essential for our well-being and safety.
4. **Actions Have Consequences**: The vulture's actions had severe

consequences not only for himself but also for his family and friends. It emphasizes the importance of considering the potential outcomes of our choices and actions.

5. **The Value of Family and Community**: The vulture's family and friends gathered to mourn his loss, highlighting the importance of family bonds and the support we find in our community during challenging times.

The Tempting Trail

Once upon a time in the great city of

Varanasi, there was a powerful king who lived in a magnificent palace surrounded by a beautiful garden. In this garden, there lived a rare and timid creature called the wind antelope. It was hardly ever seen near humans, and people believed it was impossible to capture one alive.

The king's gardener, one day, noticed the wind antelope grazing in the garden. He was amazed by this unusual sight and decided to share the news with the king. The king, curious and intrigued, asked if the gardener could capture the antelope.

The confident gardener accepted the challenge and said, "Yes, Your Majesty. I believe I can do it with a supply of honey."

The king was surprised by the gardener's plan but was willing to give him all the honey and resources he needed to achieve this feat.

The next morning, the clever gardener placed honey-coated grass in the garden, hidden from view. The wind antelope discovered the sweet treat and couldn't resist eating it. Each day, the antelope returned to enjoy more honey-coated grass.

The gardener gradually revealed himself to the antelope while feeding it honey. Eventually, the antelope grew comfortable with him, becoming addicted to the sweet honey and losing its fear of humans.

Taking advantage of this addiction, the gardener laid a trail of honey-coated grass leading to the palace. The wind antelope followed the path, and as it entered the palace, the doors were closed behind it.

Inside the unfamiliar palace, the terrified antelope tried to escape, but it was trapped. The king felt sorry for the creature, realizing how its craving and addiction had led it into a place of distress.

The king ordered his men to release the antelope and let it return to the woods. The wind antelope darted away, never to return to the palace or its gardens.

What to Learn From This Story

1. **Addiction and Craving**: The story shows how addiction and craving can lead individuals into dangerous and harmful situations. Just like the wind antelope was drawn by its addiction to honey, humans can also be trapped by their desires, losing their sense of reason.

2. **The Consequences of Ignorance**: The wind antelope's ignorance of the palace environment and the risks it posed resulted in fear and distress. This highlights the importance of being aware of one's surroundings and making informed decisions.

3. **The Power of Temptation**: Temptations, like the honey-coated grass, can lead individuals to act against their own best interests. The story reminds us to be mindful of our desires and their potential consequences.

4. **Empathy and Understanding**: The king's empathy towards the wind antelope showcases the importance of understanding and compassion

towards others, especially when they find themselves in challenging situations.

The Benevolent Ape

Once upon a time, in the hills near the great Himalaya Mountains, there lived a troop of happy monkeys. They had everything they needed and lived carefree lives. But one day, a farmer who worked nearby asked for their help. He had to go to a festival and wanted the monkeys to water his young trees while he was away.

The monkeys agreed to help and took the watering pots. However, they had no idea how to water the trees properly. Instead of watering the roots, they splashed water on the leaves. The trees didn't get the water they needed and started to wither.

While the farmer was away, he got lost in the mountains. He survived by eating sour fruit and ended up falling into a deep pit. For days, he was stuck at the bottom of the pit, hungry and desperate.

On the sixth day, a compassionate ape came to the fruit tree growing by the pit. When he heard the farmer's cries for help, he felt sorry for him. The kind ape gathered ripe fruit and tossed it to the man. Then, he decided to carry the man on his back out of the pit.

The climb was tough, and the ape struggled under the man's weight. But he didn't give up and finally made it to the top. Exhausted, the ape asked the man to keep watch while he rested.

As the man stood guard, he began to have evil thoughts. He thought that if he ate the ape, he would gain strength to find his way home. In a wicked moment, he threw a stone at the ape, but he missed and only bruised the ape's temple.

The ape was shocked and saddened by the man's actions. He couldn't understand why someone he had saved would try to harm him. Despite the man's wickedness, the compassionate ape decided to show him the way back to his village.

At the edge of the mountains, the ape told the man how to get home. Even though the man had been cruel, the ape showed compassion and warned him that his evil deeds would have consequences.

The story of the compassionate ape teaches us the importance of kindness and compassion. The ape showed kindness to the farmer, even though the farmer later turned to wickedness. It also reminds us that our actions have consequences, and being good-hearted brings goodness in return.

What to Learn From This Story

1. **Compassion and Kindness**: The ape's compassion and kindness towards the man, even after being betrayed, highlight the value of showing empathy and understanding to others.
2. **Goodness Begets Goodness**: The ape's belief that goodness returns goodness reminds us that our actions have consequences and that being kind and compassionate can lead to positive outcomes.
3. **Wickedness Begets Wickedness**: The man's wicked plan to harm the ape backfired, illustrating that negative actions can lead to negative consequences.
4. **Gratitude and Appreciation**: The story shows us the importance of being grateful for the help and kindness we

receive from others.

5. **Think Before You Act**: The man's regret after his wicked act reminds us to think carefully before we act and consider the consequences of our actions on others and ourselves.

The Clever Jackal and The Wise Rat

Once upon a time, in the lush forest around Varanasi, there were clever and friendly rats led by a wise and caring rat leader. In the same forest, a cunning jackal lived, always on the lookout for an easy meal. The jackal knew he couldn't catch the quick rats with force, so he hatched a sneaky plan.

The jackal knew the rat leader respected all things holy, so he decided to pretend to be a holy being himself. He found a path the rats often took and stood on one foot with his paws together, pretending to pray to the sun.

When the rat leader saw the peculiar sight, he was curious. He approached the jackal cautiously and asked, "Mr. Jackal, what's your name?"

"Godly is what I am called," replied the jackal smoothly.

The rat leader asked more questions, "Why do you stand on one leg?"

"If I stood on all four legs, I would be too heavy for the poor earth to bear. I don't

257

want to harm her," lied the jackal.

"And why is your mouth open?" inquired the rat.

"I only breathe the air, not wishing to hurt any living thing," answered the deceitful jackal.

"And why do you hold your paws like that and face the sun?" asked the curious rat.

"To worship and praise the sun, the giver of all life," said the false jackal.

The rat leader was deeply impressed by the supposed holiness of the jackal. He believed the jackal was a truly righteous creature from whom he and his troop could learn valuable lessons. So, from the next day onwards, the rats visited the jackal daily to show respect and listen to his teachings. But every time the rats left in an orderly line, the jackal sneakily snatched the last rat and quickly devoured him, pretending to be holy again.

As the days passed, the rat leader noticed the number of rats diminishing. He couldn't figure out why until he realized the decline began after they started visiting the jackal. He suspected the jackal was behind the disappearances.

The following day, instead of leading from the front, the rat leader took the last position when they visited the jackal. As he expected, the jackal attacked him. But the rat leader was ready. He bit the jackal's nose hard, and the jackal yelped in pain. Hearing the yelp, the other rats rushed to help their leader, chasing the jackal away.

On their way back home, the rat leader realized, "What seems to be holy is sometimes profane."

What to Learn From This Story

1. **Be cautious of appearances**: The story reminds us not to judge someone solely based on their outward appearance or claims. The rats were taken in by the jackal's pretense of holiness, which led to disastrous consequences.

2. **Critical thinking is important**:

The rat leader realized the truth behind the disappearances by observing patterns and using critical thinking. It's crucial to analyze situations and not blindly follow others.

3. **Trust must be earned**: Trust should be earned through actions and consistency, not just through words. The rats' blind trust in the jackal without verifying his intentions proved to be harmful.

4. **Be mindful of who you trust**: It's essential to be mindful of who we trust and seek advice from. In the story, the rats trusted the jackal, and it led to their troop members being harmed.

5. **Actions have consequences**: The jackal's deceitful actions had consequences for both himself and the rats. Deceptive behavior can lead to negative outcomes in the end.

6. **Avoid falling for manipulations**: The story illustrates how manipulative individuals can exploit others' trust and take advantage of them. Being aware of such manipulations can protect us from harm.

7. **Don't let emotions cloud**

judgment: The rat leader's decision to take the last position during the visit to the jackal shows that emotions like curiosity and empathy shouldn't override careful judgment.

8. **Sometimes the obvious is the best choice**: The rat leader realized that sticking to familiar ground and being cautious was the best course of action, even though it seemed less exciting or mysterious.

Overall, the story teaches us to be mindful, critical thinkers, and to exercise caution in whom we trust and follow. It also highlights the importance of seeing through deception and relying on observation and evidence.

Chasing Away A Spooky Spirit

Once upon a time, there was a man

whose wife fell terribly sick. As she lay on her deathbed, she lovingly said to her husband, "I love you so much! Promise me that you won't betray me by seeing other women after I'm gone, or I'll come back to haunt you."

After her passing, the man faithfully avoided other women for a few months, but eventually, he met someone and fell in love all over again. On the night they got engaged, the ghost of his late wife appeared before him. She blamed him for breaking his promise, and from that night on, she would return to taunt him every single night. The ghost would recount every detail of his interactions with his new fiancee, repeating their conversations word for word, which left him unable to sleep.

Feeling desperate, the man decided to seek advice from a wise Zen master who lived nearby. Upon hearing the man's tale, the master smiled and called the ghost clever. The man was puzzled but eager to know what to do.

The Zen master gave him a brilliant idea. "Next time you see the ghost," he said, "tell it that you admire its wisdom. Then, ask the ghost a question. If it answers correctly, you'll break off the engagement and remain single for life."

That night, the ghost returned as usual. Following the master's advice, the man spoke respectfully, "You are such a wise ghost! You know every little detail about me. If you can answer one question, I promise to do as you wish." The ghost was intrigued and agreed to answer the question.

The man quickly grabbed a handful of beans from a big bag on the floor and asked, "Tell me exactly how many beans there are in my hand."

In that very moment, the ghost vanished, never to return again.

And so, the man lived happily ever after, free from the haunting presence of the ghost. The lesson learned from this story is that sometimes, clever solutions can outwit even the most persistent challenges.

What to Learn From This Story

1. **Keeping promises is essential**: The man's troubles began when he broke the promise he made to his late wife. The story highlights the importance of honoring our commitments.
2. **The consequences of betrayal**: Betraying someone's trust can have significant consequences, as depicted by the haunting ghost in the story. It reminds us to be honest and faithful in our relationships.
3. **Wisdom and cleverness can be admired**: Even in difficult situations, we can find something to appreciate. The man admired the ghost's wisdom, showing that acknowledging others' strengths can be beneficial.
4. **Creative problem-solving**: The Zen master's advice demonstrated the power of creative thinking. By using a clever question, the man was able to outsmart the ghost and resolve his problem.
5. **Facing the truth**: The ghost's ability to recount every detail was a reminder that we cannot hide from the truth. Honesty and accountability are vital in

life.

6. **The power of respect**: The man's respectful approach to the ghost helped in neutralizing the haunting. Treating others with respect, even in challenging situations, can lead to better outcomes.

7. **Letting go of the past**: The story emphasizes the need to move on from past relationships and experiences. Clinging to the past can prevent us from finding happiness in the present.

8. **Seeking guidance**: The man sought help from the Zen master, illustrating the value of seeking advice and guidance when facing difficult circumstances.

9. **Overcoming fear**: Confronting the ghost with a clever question showed that facing our fears can lead to resolution and freedom from haunting thoughts.

10. **Trusting intuition**: The man followed the Zen master's advice, trusting his intuition and learning to approach the situation in a unique way.

The Wise Roshi And The Curious Student

Once upon a time, Roshi Kapleau, a Zen

master, was asked to teach a group of psycho-analysts about Zen. The director of the analytic institute introduced Roshi to the group, and he quietly sat down on a cushion placed on the floor.

A student entered the room, bowed to the master, and sat on another cushion a few feet away, facing him. Curious, the student asked, "What is Zen?" In response, the Roshi took out a banana, peeled it, and began eating.

Feeling unsatisfied with the simple demonstration, the student said, "Is that all? Can't you show me anything else?" The Roshi gestured for the student to come closer, and as the student approached, the master waved the remaining portion of the banana before his face. The student bowed and left.

Then, another student stood up and asked the audience if they understood. When no one responded, the student said, "You have just witnessed a first-rate demonstration of Zen. Any questions?"

After a long silence, one person spoke up and said, "Roshi, I am not satisfied with your demonstration. You have shown us something that I am not sure I understand. It must be possible to TELL us what Zen is."

The Roshi replied, "If you must insist on words, then Zen is an elephant copulating with a flea."

And with that enigmatic response, the Roshi left the audience to ponder the deeper meaning of Zen.

What to Learn From This Story

1. **Non-Verbal Communication**: Sometimes, words may not be enough to convey a profound message. The Roshi's demonstration using a banana and gestures exemplifies the power of non-verbal communication in conveying meaning.
2. **Experience and Understanding**: Zen and profound wisdom often come through direct experience and understanding, rather than through mere explanation or intellectualization.
3. **Open-Mindedness**: The students' reactions to the Roshi's demonstration varied. Some were content with the experience, while others sought further

clarification. It reminds us to be open-minded and receptive to different ways of learning and understanding.

4. **Simplicity in Teaching**: Profound teachings can sometimes be presented in simple and everyday actions, as demonstrated by the Roshi's act of eating a banana.

5. **Respect for Tradition**: The act of bowing and showing respect to the Roshi before and after the demonstration reflects the students' reverence for the teachings and the teacher.

6. **Humility and Patience**: The Roshi's response to the student's demand for words shows humility and patience. It highlights the value of being humble and patient in seeking wisdom and understanding.

7. **Different Perspectives**: The story illustrates how different people may interpret the same experience differently. Each student had a unique perspective on the Roshi's demonstration, emphasizing the diversity of individual experiences and insights.

8. **Emphasis on Experience**: Zen teachings often emphasize experiential learning and direct realization,

encouraging students to engage deeply in the present moment.

The Wishes Of A Dreamer

Once there was a stone cutter who felt unhappy
with his life and position. One day, as he passed

by a wealthy merchant's house, he saw all the fine possessions and important visitors, and he felt envious. "How powerful that merchant must be!" he thought.

Suddenly, he became the merchant, enjoying a life of luxury and power, but he soon realized that he was envied and detested by those less fortunate than him. Then, he saw a high official passing by, carried in a grand sedan chair with attendants and soldiers. "How powerful that official is!" he thought. "I wish I could be a high official!"

In an instant, he became the high official, being carried in an embroidered sedan chair everywhere he went. However, he found that he was feared and hated by the people around him. As he sat in the hot and sticky chair on a summer day, he looked up at the proud sun in the sky and thought, "How powerful the sun is! I wish I could be the sun!"

And just like that, he became the sun, shining fiercely and scorching the fields, only to be cursed by the farmers and laborers. But then a huge black cloud moved in, blocking his light. "How powerful that storm cloud is! I wish I could be a cloud!" he thought.

So, he became the cloud, flooding the fields and

villages and being shouted at by everyone. But soon, he felt a great force pushing him away, and he realized it was the wind. "How powerful it is! I wish I could be the wind!" he thought.

And there he was, the wind, blowing tiles off roofs and uprooting trees, feared and hated by all below him. But as he continued blowing, he came across a huge, towering rock that wouldn't budge. "How powerful that rock is! I wish I could be a rock!" he thought.

And just like that, he became the rock, feeling more powerful than anything else on earth. But then he heard the sound of a hammer and chisel pounding into the hard surface. He looked down and saw a stone cutter shaping him.

He realized that even though he was the rock, he wasn't the most powerful after all. There was always something or someone greater. He learned that contentment and acceptance of who he was would bring him true happiness, rather than constantly wanting to be something else.

In the end, he understood that being a simple stone cutter was not a position to be envious of, but a humble and satisfying one. He finally found peace and happiness with himself as the stone cutter, knowing that true power lies in accepting oneself as one is.

What to Learn From This Story

1. **Gratitude and Contentment**: The stone cutter's journey through different roles shows the importance of being grateful for what we have. Each time he wished to be something else, he realized that there were drawbacks and challenges in every position. Learning to appreciate and be content with our current circumstances can bring greater happiness.

2. **Mindfulness and Perspective**: As the stone cutter experienced various roles, he gained perspective on the different aspects of life. This teaches us the value of mindfulness and stepping back to see things from different angles. It helps us avoid rash decisions driven by envy or desire.

3. **Pursuit of Power**: The stone cutter's desire to be more powerful led him from one position to another, but he found that power alone doesn't guarantee happiness. It shows us that chasing power for its own sake can lead to dissatisfaction and loss of true identity.

4. **Humility and Acceptance**: The story demonstrates the importance of humility and acceptance. Despite being a powerful figure like the sun, cloud, and wind, the stone cutter found peace and contentment

when he accepted his role as a simple stone cutter. Accepting ourselves and others as we are can lead to inner peace.

5. **The Ever-Present Change**: The story highlights the impermanence of life. The stone cutter's constant transformations remind us that life is constantly changing, and nothing is permanent. Embracing change and staying adaptable can help us navigate life's challenges.

6. **Focus on What Truly Matters**: In the end, the stone cutter realized that seeking power and greatness didn't bring lasting happiness. It is a reminder to focus on the things that truly matter in life, such as love, compassion, and self-awareness.

7. **Be Grateful for Simplicity**: The story celebrates the beauty and fulfillment that can be found in simple roles and ordinary lives. Sometimes, it's the most straightforward things that bring the most joy and satisfaction.

The Spider's Lesson

In a remote Tibetan monastery, a young

meditation student faced a peculiar challenge. Every time he meditated in his room, he believed he saw a menacing spider descending in front of him. Each day, the spider seemed to grow larger and more terrifying. Frightened and desperate, he decided to seek guidance from his wise teacher.

The student approached his teacher and explained the distressing situation. He declared his intention to place a knife in his lap during meditation, so that when the spider appeared, he could kill it and rid himself of the fear. However, the teacher, with serene wisdom, advised against such a violent plan.

Instead, the teacher offered a unique suggestion. He handed the student a piece of chalk and said, "Take this to your meditation, and when the spider appears, mark an 'X' on its belly. Then come back to me."

Intrigued by this curious advice, the student followed the teacher's words. During his next meditation session, as the spider materialized once again, he resisted the urge to attack it. Instead, he gently marked an "X" on its belly using the chalk.

Later, the student returned to his teacher and recounted his experience. The teacher smiled and said, "Now, lift up your shirt and look at your own belly."

To his astonishment, there on his own belly was the unmistakable "X." The student realized the profound lesson his teacher had taught him. The menacing spider was merely a reflection of his own fears and insecurities.

What to Learn From This Story

1. **Self-Awareness**: The story emphasizes the importance of self-awareness. The meditation student's fear of the spider represents his inner fears and insecurities. By recognizing and understanding these emotions, we can gain insights into ourselves and our reactions to external situations.

2. **Mindfulness**: The teacher's advice to mark an "X" on the spider's belly with chalk encourages mindfulness. Instead of reacting impulsively to fear, the student learns to observe his feelings without judgment. Mindfulness helps us stay present in the moment and respond thoughtfully to challenges.

3. **Confronting Fears**: Rather than avoiding or attacking his fear, the student confronts it in a non-harmful way.

Confronting our fears allows us to address and overcome them, leading to personal growth and empowerment.

4. **Perceptions and Projection**: The spider being a reflection of the student's fears highlights how our perceptions and projections shape our experiences. The world around us often mirrors our inner thoughts and feelings, reminding us to be mindful of our thoughts and attitudes.

5. **Non-Violence**: The teacher's advice to avoid killing the spider promotes non-violence and compassion. Violence, whether physical or emotional, seldom resolves our issues and may lead to negative consequences.

6. **Seek Wisdom from Others**: The student sought guidance from his wise teacher, and this led him to a deeper understanding of himself. Seeking counsel and learning from others can be valuable in navigating life's challenges.

7. **Internal Solutions**: The story encourages us to look within ourselves for solutions to our problems. It reminds us that our actions, attitudes, and perceptions influence our experiences and

how we handle them.

8. **Letting Go of Fear**: By facing his fear and realizing its nature, the student learns to let go of the grip fear had on him. This demonstrates the power of understanding and acceptance in alleviating fear's impact on our lives.

The Wise Turtle And The Greedy Monkeys:

Once upon a time, in a magical forest, there

lived a group of playful and mischievous monkeys. Among them was a wise old turtle named Kavi, who had a cozy home in a sparkling pond. The monkeys loved playing near the pond and often teased Kavi for being slow.

One sunny day, the monkeys gathered around the pond and started poking fun at Kavi. "Hey, slowpoke turtle! You can't even climb trees like us!" giggled one of the monkeys.

Another monkey chimed in, "Yeah! You're soooo slow!"

Kavi, the wise turtle, smiled kindly and said, "Dear monkeys, even though I'm not fast like you, I have seen many wonderful things in my long life."

But the monkeys just laughed and didn't listen to the wise turtle's words. They loved their quick moves and didn't think they needed any advice.

Then, one curious and daring monkey named Raja had an idea. "Hey, Kavi, if you're so smart, tell us the fastest way to get to the other side of the forest!" challenged Raja.

Kavi thought for a moment and replied, "The fastest way is to work together as a team. Help each other and you'll find the quickest path!"

The monkeys giggled and rolled their eyes. They thought running and jumping on their own was much faster than working together.

Ignoring Kavi's advice, the monkeys raced into the forest, each trying to be the fastest. They swung from trees and hopped from branch to branch, but something unexpected happened. They got lost!

As the sun began to set, the monkeys felt tired and scared. Raja felt bad for not listening to Kavi's wise words.

"We're lost, and it's all my fault!" Raja said with a frown.

Just then, Kavi came to the rescue, slowly but surely. He found the monkeys and gently said, "Don't worry, my friends. It's never too late to learn. Let's work together to find the way back."

The monkeys listened carefully this time. They followed Kavi's guidance and helped each other find their way through the forest.

With Kavi's wisdom and the monkeys' teamwork, they finally reached the other side just as the moon rose in the sky.

From that day on, the monkeys admired Kavi's wisdom and thanked him for saving them. They learned the value of cooperation and kindness, and they all became great friends with the wise old turtle.

And so, in the magical forest, the monkeys and Kavi, the wise turtle, lived happily ever after, sharing adventures and learning together as a team.

What to Learn From This Story

1. **Wisdom and Knowledge**: The story teaches us that wisdom and knowledge are valuable traits. Just like the wise turtle, Kavi, who had seen many things in his long life, learning from experience and being patient can help us make better decisions.

2. **Humility**: The monkeys' initial pride and arrogance led them to make mistakes and get lost. Being humble and open to learning from others, regardless of their appearance or abilities, can lead to better outcomes.

3. **Cooperation and Teamwork**: Working together as a team can achieve great things. The monkeys learned that unity and helping one another can lead to success, just as they found their way back with Kavi's guidance and support.

4. **Listening and Learning**: It's essential to listen to advice, especially from those who are wiser and more experienced. Ignoring valuable insights can lead to challenges, but being open to learning from others can lead to growth and better decisions.

5. **Kindness and Friendship**: Being kind to others and treating them with respect can build lasting friendships. The monkeys' friendship with Kavi grew stronger as they appreciated his wisdom and learned from his guidance.

6. **Patience**: The wise turtle, Kavi, showed patience and understanding towards the monkeys, even when they mocked him. Patience allows us to

remain calm in difficult situations and make thoughtful choices.

7. **Apologizing and Taking Responsibility**: When the young monkey, Raja, realized his mistake, he apologized and took responsibility for their situation. Admitting our mistakes and learning from them is a crucial part of growing as individuals.

The Compassionate Elephant And The Injured Bird

In a vast jungle, there lived a majestic and kind-hearted elephant named Gagan. He was known for his gentle nature and compassion towards all living beings. One day, as Gagan was strolling through the forest, he heard a faint cry for help. Following the sound, he discovered a wounded bird lying on the forest floor. The little bird had a broken wing and couldn't fly.

Filled with empathy, Gagan carefully picked up the injured bird with his trunk and placed it gently on his broad back. He promised to take care of the bird until it healed and could fly again.

As the days passed, Gagan made sure the bird had enough food and water. He found a safe and cozy spot for the bird to rest. Despite his enormous size, Gagan handled the fragile creature with utmost care and tenderness.

During their time together, the bird shared stories of the world it had seen from high up in the sky. It spoke of distant lands, breathtaking sights, and the freedom of flying among the clouds. Gagan listened intently, captivated by the bird's tales.

One evening, while the bird was resting on Gagan's back, it said, "Thank you, dear Gagan, for your kindness and compassion. You could have easily ignored a little bird like me, but you chose to help and befriend me."

Gagan replied, "It is my duty to protect and care for those in need. We are all interconnected in this vast web of life, and it is essential to extend our love and support to one another."

As weeks passed, the bird's wing gradually healed, and it was ready to fly again. The bird looked at Gagan with gratitude in its eyes and said, "I wish I could repay your kindness, dear Gagan. Is there anything I can do for you?"

Gagan smiled and replied, "Your recovery and friendship are enough for me, little one. But if you insist, please remember the value of compassion and extend it to others in need. Let your wings carry not only your body but also the message of love and care for all creatures."

With tears of joy, the bird promised to follow Gagan's advice and set out into the open sky.

From that day on, it traveled to different places, helping injured animals and spreading the message of compassion wherever it went.

As for Gagan, his act of kindness and the bond he formed with the bird brought him immense happiness. He continued to roam the jungle, always ready to help any creature in distress, and his compassionate nature touched the hearts of all who encountered him.

And so, the story of the compassionate elephant, Gagan, and the grateful bird became a cherished tale among the animals of the jungle, inspiring them to show kindness and empathy to one another.

What to Learn From This Story

1. **Compassion and Kindness**: Gagan, the elephant, shows us the importance of compassion and kindness towards all living beings. His willingness to help the injured bird without hesitation demonstrates the power of empathy and how small acts of kindness can make a significant difference in

someone's life.

2. **Helping Others in Need**: Gagan's act of caring for the injured bird reminds us of the value of helping those in need. It encourages us to extend a helping hand to others and offer support and assistance whenever we can.

3. **Interconnectedness of Life**: The story emphasizes the interconnectedness of all living creatures in the web of life. Gagan's understanding of this concept leads him to show love and care to the injured bird, acknowledging that every being deserves compassion and respect.

4. **Gratitude**: The injured bird expresses its gratitude towards Gagan for his help and friendship. Gratitude is a powerful emotion that fosters positivity and strengthens relationships between individuals.

5. **Sharing Stories and Wisdom**: Through the bird's tales of its experiences, we learn the value of sharing stories and wisdom with others. Listening to each other's experiences can be enlightening and foster a sense of understanding and appreciation for the world around us.

6. **Leading by Example**: Gagan leads by example, demonstrating the importance of being compassionate and caring towards others. His actions inspire the bird to follow his teachings and spread the message of love and compassion to others.

7. **Empowerment through Support**: Gagan's support and care empower the injured bird to recover and help others in need. It reminds us that sometimes a little support and encouragement can give someone the strength to overcome challenges and make a positive impact.

8. **Cherishing Nature**: The story takes place in a jungle, reminding us of the beauty and wonder of nature. It encourages us to appreciate and cherish the natural world and the diverse creatures that inhabit it.

The Grateful Mouse And The Kind Farmer

In a quaint village surrounded by fields of golden wheat, there lived a kind-hearted farmer named Anand. He toiled day and night, working on his farm to provide food for his family and the entire village. The villagers admired Anand for his generosity and compassion.

One sunny morning, as Anand was plowing the fields, he accidentally turned over a mouse's nest with his plow. Inside the nest were tiny baby mice, frightened and helpless. Feeling sorry for the little creatures, Anand gently picked them up and placed them in a safe spot away from harm.

Among the baby mice was a tiny, grateful mouse named Chiku. He was touched by the farmer's act of kindness and wanted to show his gratitude. So, as soon as he was old enough, Chiku decided to repay Anand's kindness.

Every night, after Anand had gone to bed, Chiku sneaked into the farmer's barn and nibbled on any pests that were damaging the crops. He ate the harmful insects, keeping the crops safe from infestations and ensuring a bountiful harvest for Anand.

As the days passed, Anand noticed that his crops were healthier and more abundant than ever before. He couldn't figure out the reason behind the sudden improvement, but he was grateful for the miracle that seemed to be happening.

One night, unable to contain his curiosity any longer, Anand decided to stay awake and investigate the mystery. To his surprise, he saw the tiny Chiku working diligently, protecting his crops from pests.

Amazed and touched by the little mouse's efforts, Anand smiled and said, "Thank you, little one, for your help and dedication. You are a true friend to me and a blessing to this farm."

Chiku, feeling grateful for Anand's words, replied, "It was you who saved my life and the lives of my siblings when you saved us from the overturned nest. It is my honor and duty to repay your kindness by protecting your crops."

From that day on, Chiku continued to be the farmer's loyal companion, guarding the crops at night and keeping them safe from harm. Anand and Chiku formed a deep bond of friendship and understanding.

Word of the miraculous mouse that protected the farmer's crops spread throughout the village. The villagers praised Anand's kindness, and they, too, started treating the mice in their fields with more care and compassion.

The story of the grateful mouse and the kind farmer became a legend in the village, reminding everyone that even the smallest acts of kindness can have a significant impact and lead to unexpected friendships. Anand and Chiku's story taught the villagers the value of compassion and gratitude, making the village a place filled with warmth and harmony.

What to Learn From This Story

1. **Kindness Begets Kindness**: Anand's act of saving the baby mice's lives led to Chiku's gratitude and his willingness to repay the kindness by protecting the farmer's crops. It reminds us that acts of kindness can

inspire others to be kind in return.

2. **Gratitude and Reciprocity**: Chiku's gratitude towards Anand shows the importance of being thankful for the help and kindness we receive. Gratitude can lead us to reciprocate and give back when the opportunity arises.

3. **Unexpected Friendships**: Anand and Chiku, a farmer and a tiny mouse, formed an unlikely but beautiful friendship. The story reminds us that friendships can be found in the most unexpected places, transcending differences in size, species, or background.

4. **The Power of Compassion**: Anand's compassion towards the baby mice had a positive ripple effect on the entire village. The villagers learned to treat the mice in their fields with more care and compassion, fostering a harmonious environment.

5. **Appreciating Small Acts**: The story emphasizes that even the smallest acts of kindness, like saving a tiny mouse's life, can have a significant impact on others and create a chain of positive actions.

6. **Curiosity and Understanding**: Anand's curiosity to understand the

mystery behind the improved crops allowed him to discover Chiku's nightly efforts. It highlights the value of curiosity and understanding in building relationships and appreciating others' efforts.

7. **Gratitude's Ripple Effect**: The gratitude shown by Anand and Chiku's actions had a ripple effect on the entire village, inspiring others to be kind and considerate as well. This reminds us of the power of gratitude to create a positive and harmonious community.

8. **Protecting Nature**: Chiku's role as a pest controller in the farmer's barn teaches us about the importance of respecting and protecting nature. It shows how a balanced ecosystem benefits everyone, including humans and animals.

9. **Value of Friendship**: The story emphasizes the value of true friendship, where both parties care for and support each other. Anand and Chiku's friendship is based on mutual respect, trust, and appreciation.

10. **Lessons from Unlikely Sources**: The villagers learned valuable lessons from a tiny mouse and a

kind farmer. It reminds us to be open to learning from unlikely sources and to appreciate the wisdom found in unexpected places.

The Selfless Deer And The Hunter's Trap

In a peaceful forest, there lived a selfless deer named Manohar. He was famous for his caring nature and his willingness to help others in need. One day, while exploring the forest, Manohar stumbled upon a hunter's trap cunningly concealed among the bushes. Realizing the danger it posed to other animals, he decided to warn them.

Manohar gathered all the forest animals and alerted them about the trap. He said, "Hey, there's a hunter's trap hidden near those bushes. Be careful while moving through this area, and let's look out for each other to avoid this danger."

The animals were grateful for Manohar's warning and admired his selflessness. They decided to put up a sign near the trap to warn others and came up with a plan to protect each other from such dangers in the future.

Manohar's kind and caring actions earned him admiration and respect throughout the forest. He became a beloved leader among the animals, and they all lived harmoniously, watching out for each other's safety.

What to Learn From This Story

1. **Selflessness and Kindness**: The story teaches us the value of selflessness and kindness. Manohar, the deer, demonstrates the importance of caring for others and being willing to help those in need without expecting anything in return.

2. **Responsibility and Leadership**: Manohar takes responsibility for the well-being of the other animals in the forest by warning them about the hunter's trap. His actions show that true leadership involves looking out for the safety and welfare of the community.

3. **Cooperation and Teamwork**: The animals in the forest come together and work as a team to protect each other from dangers. They show the significance of cooperation and unity in overcoming challenges and ensuring the safety of everyone.

4. **Gratitude and Respect**: The animals in the forest are grateful to Manohar for his warning and admire his selflessness. The story highlights the importance of showing gratitude and

respect to those who help and support us.

5. **Awareness and Caution**: The story emphasizes the importance of being aware of potential dangers in our surroundings and taking caution to avoid them. By being vigilant, we can protect ourselves and others from harm.

6. **Leading by Example**: Manohar's actions inspire the other animals to take similar measures in protecting each other. The story reminds us that leading by example can have a positive impact on others and encourage them to do good as well.

7. **Compassion for All Living Beings**: The story promotes compassion for all living beings, regardless of their species. It encourages us to treat animals with care and respect, acknowledging their role in maintaining the balance of nature.

8. **Problem-Solving and Prevention**: The animals' decision to put up a sign near the trap shows the importance of proactive problem-solving and prevention. They take steps to avoid future accidents and ensure the safety of everyone in the forest.

The Patient Tortoise And The Hasty Hare

In a different part of the forest, there lived a boastful hare named Harsha, who was known for his incredible speed. He often boasted about how fast he was and ridiculed the slower animals, particularly the tortoise, Tanmay.

One day, Tanmay couldn't bear Harsha's taunts any longer and challenged him to a race. Harsha, filled with pride, readily agreed, thinking it would be an easy victory for him. The race was set, and the entire forest gathered to watch.

As the race began, Harsha sprinted ahead, leaving Tanmay far behind. Confident of his imminent win, Harsha decided to take a nap under a shady tree. Meanwhile, Tanmay continued to move slowly but steadily, never losing sight of the finish line.

When Harsha woke up and saw Tanmay nearing the end, he rushed to catch up, but it was too late. The patient tortoise had crossed the finish line, winning the race.

Humiliated and ashamed of his arrogance, Harsha apologized to Tanmay for underestimating him. He learned a valuable lesson that day – that patience and determination could lead to success, even when faced with seemingly faster opponents.

What to Learn From This Story

1. **Don't Underestimate Others:** Harsha's arrogance led him to underestimate Tanmay's abilities. The story reminds us to respect others and not judge them based on appearances or preconceived notions.
2. **Patience Pays Off:** Tanmay's patient and steady approach helped him achieve his goal. The story emphasizes the importance of patience and perseverance in overcoming challenges.
3. **Avoiding Overconfidence:** Harsha's overconfidence led to his downfall. It's essential to be confident in one's abilities, but not to the extent that it blinds us to potential obstacles or competitors.
4. **Learn from Mistakes:** Harsha's realization of his mistake and apology demonstrate the importance of acknowledging and learning from our errors. It's okay to make mistakes, but the key is to grow and improve from them.

The Curious Crow And The Enchanted Forest:

In the heart of the forest, there lived a curious crow named Kamal. He was always inquisitive and eager to explore new places. One day, he heard a rumor about an enchanted forest hidden deep within the woods. Intrigued by the idea of an enchanted place, Kamal set out on a quest to find it.

After days of flying and exploring, Kamal stumbled upon the entrance to the enchanted forest. As he entered, he was mesmerized by the beauty and magic that surrounded him. The trees sparkled with enchanting lights, and the animals spoke in a language he could understand.

Kamal spent days exploring the magical forest, but he soon realized that the enchantment had a price. Every animal in the forest seemed content and happy, but they had lost their freedom to leave. The magic was so enticing that they were afraid to venture outside the enchanted borders.

Feeling a sense of responsibility, Kamal decided to share his discovery with the animals outside the forest. He believed that true freedom and happiness lie in embracing life's challenges and not being bound by magical illusions.

He returned to his fellow crows and the other animals in the forest and shared his experiences. Though some were tempted, they eventually realized the wisdom of Kamal's words. They chose to live freely, cherishing the natural beauty of the forest around them without being confined by an illusion of enchantment.

What to Learn From This Story

1. **Curiosity and Exploration**: Kamal's curiosity led him to discover the enchanted forest. The story encourages children to embrace their curiosity and explore the world around them to make exciting discoveries.
2. **The Price of Enchantment**: While the enchanted forest seemed magical and alluring, it came with a price - the loss of freedom. It teaches children to be cautious of things that might seem attractive but could have undesirable consequences.
3. **True Freedom and Happiness**: The story highlights the importance of true freedom and happiness, which comes

from facing life's challenges and not being confined by illusions or artificial happiness.

4. **Wisdom and Responsibility**: Kamal's decision to share his discovery with others demonstrates wisdom and responsibility. The story encourages children to share knowledge and experiences for the greater good.

5. **Embrace Nature's Beauty**: The animals in the forest learned to cherish the natural beauty around them without being bound by illusions. It emphasizes the beauty of the real world and appreciating nature's wonders.

The Devoted Dog And The Wandering Monk:

In a peaceful village, there lived a devoted dog named Bheema. He was known for his loyalty and affection towards his owner, a wandering monk named Siddharth. Siddharth had renounced worldly possessions and lived a life of simplicity, traveling from place to place to spread teachings of peace and compassion.

Bheema followed Siddharth everywhere he went, serving and protecting him throughout his journeys. He was not only a loyal companion but also a source of comfort for the monk during times of solitude.

One day, as they traveled through a dense forest, they encountered a ferocious wild animal. Siddharth, being a peaceful monk, refused to harm the creature and instead recited prayers for its well-being. Bheema, seeing the danger, bravely stood between the monk and the wild animal, ready to defend him at any cost.

Moved by Bheema's loyalty and courage, the wild animal eventually calmed down and left peacefully. Siddharth realized the depth of Bheema's devotion and said, "You are not just a dog, dear Bheema. You are a true embodiment of love and protection. Your loyalty humbles me, and I am grateful for your presence in my life."

From that day on, Siddharth and Bheema continued their journey together, spreading the message of love and devotion wherever they went. Their bond became an inspiration to many, teaching the value of selfless love and loyalty in all relationships.

And so, the stories of these fascinating Buddhist animal tales enriched the lives of those who heard them, instilling valuable life lessons and moral teachings for generations to come.

What to Learn From This Story

1. **Loyalty and Devotion**: Bheema's unwavering loyalty and devotion to his owner, Siddharth, demonstrate the power of unconditional love and dedication in relationships. It teaches us the importance of being faithful and committed to those we care about.
2. **Compassion and Non-violence**: Siddharth's refusal to harm the wild animal and his prayers for its well-being

showcase the virtues of compassion and non-violence. It reminds us to approach challenging situations with empathy and a peaceful attitude.

3. **Bravery and Protection**: Bheema's courage in standing between Siddharth and the ferocious animal exemplifies the value of bravery and protection. It shows that we should be willing to stand up for those we love, even in the face of danger.

4. **Gratitude and Appreciation**: Siddharth's expression of gratitude towards Bheema for his loyalty highlights the importance of recognizing and appreciating the love and support we receive from others.

5. **The Power of Love**: The deep bond between Siddharth and Bheema exemplifies the transformative power of love. It illustrates how love can bridge the gap between species and create meaningful connections.

6. **Life's True Purpose**: Siddharth and Bheema's journey together to spread teachings of peace and compassion signifies the significance of living a purposeful life and making a positive impact on others.

7. **Interconnectedness**: The story emphasizes the interconnectedness of all living beings and the significance of treating every creature with respect and kindness.

The Sacred Lotus and the Curious Squirrel

In a pristine glade filled with lush vegetation and adorned by a tranquil pond, resided a sacred lotus. Its bloom held an ethereal allure, untouched by the muddy water from which it sprouted. The beauty of this lotus, solitary in its elegant repose, captivated a curious squirrel.

This vivacious creature, known for its constant scurrying and boundless energy, was inexplicably drawn to the tranquil lotus. One day, with a heart full of curiosity, the squirrel decided to approach the lotus. He asked, "Oh, wise Lotus, in your silence, you embody a tranquility I struggle to understand. I gather and store, I run and explore, while you remain still and content. How do you find such peace?"

The lotus, undisturbed by the surrounding elements, replied in a soft, soothing voice, "Little Squirrel, we live in the same world but perceive it differently. I embrace my circumstances, remain firmly rooted, yet detached from my muddy origins. I bask in the present and grow from my center outwards. You, my friend, seek and store, always anticipating the future, never truly here in the now."

What to Learn From This Story

This charming tale of the sacred lotus and the curious squirrel offers profound lessons on mindfulness, gratitude, and happiness.

The principle of mindfulness emphasizes the power of the present moment. The lotus, grounded in the mud yet rising above the water, is a testament to the ability to live in the now. Despite its murky surroundings, it focuses on its present state of being, blooming in full glory. The squirrel's question highlights a common struggle to comprehend this tranquility amidst apparent chaos. This underlines the importance of mindfulness – the ability to live in the present moment, acknowledging but not consumed by one's circumstances.

Gratitude can be observed in the lotus's acceptance of its surroundings. It grows from the mud, accepting its origin, and deriving nourishment from it. This embodies an expression of gratitude for the circumstances that contribute to growth, however unfavorable they may seem. We, too, can cultivate gratitude by acknowledging the value in our experiences, recognizing them as stepping stones towards growth and self-improvement.

Finally, the pursuit of happiness is a central theme. The lotus radiates joy not from external conditions but from its inner state. It stands as a symbol of deriving contentment and joy from the present, from 'being' rather than 'doing'. On the other hand, the squirrel, always in motion, never quite settles to appreciate the present moment, which can be a source of genuine happiness. This reminds us to seek happiness not in anticipation of future gains but in the peaceful acceptance and appreciation of the present.

The Hermit and the Lotus Flower

Nestled in the heart of a thick forest, a venerable hermit lived a life of solitude. His existence was marked by simple needs and the company of the vibrant flora and fauna around him. Among all the marvels of nature he witnessed each day, one humble lotus flower growing by the nearby pond fascinated him the most.

Day by day, he would observe the lotus flower's progression from a bud to a beautiful bloom. This transformation occurred against all odds - from the muddy, murky depths, the lotus always emerged, pure and untainted. Its serene beauty against such challenging circumstances intrigued the hermit, and he contemplated the profound lesson it offered.

One day, the hermit shared his observations with a passing traveler. "Every morning, this lotus flower emerges from the muddy pond, maintaining its purity and radiating beauty. Despite the darkness at the bottom of the pond, it blooms unblemished, showing us that we, too, can rise above our challenges and bloom in our true nature."

What to Learn From This Story

This tale of the hermit and the lotus flower carries significant wisdom about mindfulness, gratitude, and the pursuit of genuine happiness.

The mindfulness principle is embodied in the hermit's keen observation of the lotus flower's journey from bud to bloom. Instead of dwelling on the past or future, the hermit lives in the present, closely observing the world around him. His attention to the lotus flower's daily transformation is a practice of mindfulness - fully engaged with and attentive to the present moment.

The story also speaks of gratitude. The lotus flower, despite growing in murky waters, blooms each day with renewed beauty, symbolizing an acceptance of and gratitude for its circumstances. Similarly, the hermit expresses gratitude by appreciating the natural wonder and teachings of the lotus flower. This tale encourages us to be grateful for our conditions, as they mold us into who we are.

The narrative finally imparts a lesson on happiness. The lotus flower's ability to rise and bloom from the muddy pond mirrors our potential to find happiness within ourselves, despite our circumstances. Happiness, as the hermit implies, is not dependent on external factors but rather on our inner state of being. In the same vein, the hermit's solitary yet contented life illustrates the pursuit of inner happiness, devoid of materialistic distractions.

The Dragonfly and the Whispering Lotus

In a serene and secluded forest, on the edge of a peaceful pond, resided a vibrant dragonfly. This forest was also home to a blossoming lotus flower that held a unique ability - it could whisper the wisdom of the ages. The dragonfly, unlike his kind, wasn't a fleeting visitor. He chose to stay close to the whispering lotus, enchanted by its wisdom and beauty.

Day after day, the dragonfly would flutter around the lotus, drawn by the soft whispers of wisdom that echoed across the serene waters. The lotus spoke of embracing change, of the transient nature of life, and the beauty that lies therein. It also narrated stories of its journey from a tiny seed in the mud to a radiant bloom on the water's surface, unaffected by the murkiness it was born into.

One day, a tired sparrow happened upon the dragonfly and the whispering lotus. Noticing the rapt attention the dragonfly gave to the lotus, the sparrow asked, "Why do you spend your days buzzing around this flower when there are miles of forest to explore?"

To this, the dragonfly replied, "Each day with the whispering lotus is a journey of discovery. In its whispers, I've learned to cherish every fleeting moment and found happiness within the constant flux of life."

What to Learn From This Story

The tale of the dragonfly and the whispering lotus provides essential lessons about mindfulness, gratitude, and the pursuit of true happiness.

Mindfulness is manifested through the dragonfly's focused attention on the lotus' whispers. He lives fully in each moment, not fluttering mindlessly but absorbing the wisdom around him. His mindful presence allows him to appreciate the lotus' teachings, reflecting the power of being wholly engaged in the present.

The story also subtly teaches gratitude. The lotus, despite its muddy beginnings, grows into a beautiful flower, emitting wisdom and serenity. This transformation is a metaphor for appreciating and being grateful for life's challenges, as they contribute to our growth. The dragonfly, too, displays gratitude by valuing the lotus' wisdom and the enriching experiences it provides.

Finally, this narrative shares a profound understanding of happiness. The dragonfly, spending his days around the whispering lotus, finds happiness not in material things but in the intangible wisdom imparted by the lotus. The story conveys that true happiness is a state of being that arises from within, and it is attainable irrespective of our external circumstances, as evidenced by the radiant lotus thriving in the muddy pond.

Printed in the USA
CPSIA information can be obtained
at www.ICGtesting.com
LVHW021105031023
759761LV00074B/1570